Mommy, they're taking away my imagination!

Educating Your Young Child At Home

Pam Oken-Wright

Mommy, they're taking away my imagination!
Educating Your Young Child At Home

Layout and Design by Andy Grachuk
www.JingotheCat.com

Dedicated to Tristan James Wright, my son and inspiration

Table of Contents

Preface: A Child's Way of Being in the World

I was working at my desk on the sun porch, with the sliding glass door open and rain pouring onto the courtyard beyond. My three-year-old son pressed his hands to the screen and was still long enough that, intrigued, I looked up from my work.

"Mommy," he said, turning to face me. "I know how it rains."

"You do?" I invited.

"Yes," he said. "The flowers drink, and then they spit the water up into the sky. Then the sky keeps the water until it rains."

Since he was used to my soliciting his theories about how things work, my son knew how to articulate his theory, and he knew the pleasure of doing so. As a result, I got to be witness to this—and a thousand more—moments of brilliance.

In addition to being Tristan's mom, I taught four- to six-year-olds for nearly four decades. For three of those decades, my classroom practice was inspired by the schools of Reggio Emilia. As a teacher-researcher in a Reggio-inspired classroom, I learned from the hundreds of young children I'd known to expect to be left in awe when in the presence of their thinking. If you listen to your child as much as you talk, if you ask as much as you tell, you, too, will be amazed at the power of your child's intellect.

Every child is intelligent, resourceful, competent, and driven toward relationship with other people and the world. But not every child grows up believing this about himself. Not every child is invited to show these things to the world. These days, academic proficiency takes center stage in school, even preschool sometimes, and your child's intellect—the way he thinks about the world and himself—and growth of personal resources that help a child know how to learn get second billing if they are considered at all.

You are your child's teacher. You were her first teacher, you are her forever teacher. Perhaps you are collaborating with school, which is wonderful. This book can help your home and school become an extension of each other. But perhaps you are just observing your child's schooling. Perhaps school told you, "We'll take it from here." So many parents feel they must trust the system, whether or not what happens in school on a daily basis feels right to them. And many parents don't know that there could be a way other than the way they themselves learned in school. A way that fits the combination of a child and the world he lives in. A way that does more than try to fill a child's head with facts and his mind with discrete skills. Facts and skills are no longer enough. Necessary…just not sufficient.

This book is for parents of young children educating at home, whether instead of school or in addition to school. And it is for teachers of young children who want another way of thinking about early childhood education and how they can collaborate with parents or who already have another way of thinking but want more resources. It is for anyone who has a role in growing a curious, resourceful, thoughtful human being. My hope is that you will take what is of use to you, make it your own, extrapolate, imagine, and invent. And maybe you will rediscover your own curiosity and imagination in the process.

"Education is the kindling of a flame, not the filling of a vessel."

- Socrates

1 What is Education and What is Learning?

Schooling is what we have come to understand as the goal of going to school. Too often, schooling means learning what they tell me to learn, memorizing, and figuring out what the teacher wants. But "education," from the Latin "educare," to draw out, is something else. The educated individual has learned how to think, to solve problems, to invent, to consider alternatives, to persist, to create, to innovate, and to articulate her thinking. On the other hand, education is the "leading forth" of my potential as a whole. I hope that as you read this book you will not only understand but come to cherish that potential in your child. That as your child finds her voice and articulates her theories about how the world works and shows you the symbolic thinking of which she is capable, you will embrace the difference between schooling and education. This book is here so that you can accompany your child on her childhood journey in a new way.

In forty years of teaching four- to six-year-old children, I learned that the knowledge that sticks and what makes a person a lifelong learner are much bigger than the list of facts and skills that make up most school curricula. Yes, knowing things is important. But in order to really know something, there has to be a framework within which those facts and skills reside. That framework is made up of dispositions toward learning, habits of mind, and the knowledge the child himself has constructed previously.

How Learning Occurs

Receiving information — hearing it, reading it, or experiencing it — is not learning. Information is necessary for learning but is only part of the process. In order for me to learn, I have to do something with what I have heard/ seen/experienced. I have to construct knowledge. I have to change my understanding and thinking a little to accommodate the new information. For example, say your toddler knows about dogs: four legs, a tail, fur. This is his experience of, and understanding of, a dog. He has an imaginary mental box for "dog." Then one day, you go on a car ride in the country and you pass a field of cows. Your child sees a cow and says, "Dog!" The cow has fit his criteria for a dog: four legs, a tail, and fur. You say, "No, honey, that is a cow." Your child then has to alter his mental image of "dog." He has to figure out how the cow is different from a dog. Now, in his mind, there are two categories where there once was one; he now has both a mental cow "box" and a dog "box." And you have observed learning. You can tell him this animal is "cow" and this animal is "dog," but you are only giving names to what the learner must construct in his own mind.

Dispositions and Habits of Mind

Dispositions are emotional stances or desires. Someone who has a positive disposition toward learning will always be eager to learn and will seek out experiences that will result in learning. If you love learning, chances are you have the disposition to:

- Be aware of your own curiosity and are inclined to follow it
- Collaborate with others
- Solve problems
- Seek challenges
- Represent/articulate your ideas. You expect to and trust that you can express your ideas in many different ways.
- Innovate and invent
- Be a protagonist in your own learning
- Find joy in learning

Habits of mind are practiced skills that allow us to satisfy our dispositions toward learning. They may include:

- Persisting. You invest increasing amounts of time and energy on what interests you.

- Pursuing a question or a problem

- Engaging in inquiry. If you want to know, you explore or experiment to find out.

- Reflecting. You engage in reflection on your own process, for example, "Why did my block building fall down?"

- Representing ideas with growing detail and accuracy

  ○ You use a variety of media to explore and express ideas.

  ○ You develop and continue to hone a reasonable "satisfaction bar."

  ○ You use many different media and modalities to clarify your point of view and communicate it to others.

- Engaging in conversation about how the world works

  ○ You articulate your own hypotheses and theories.

  ○ You listen to the ideas of others and consider multiple perspectives in working toward a shared goal.

- Inviting others to collaborate. You participate in the informal exchange of ideas verbally and through symbolic representation, such as drawing and constructing.

- Engaging in flexible thinking. For example, if plan A doesn't work, you can imagine plan B.

- Developing an "awake mind"

When a child has developed these dispositions and habits of mind, learning becomes a more natural process, for which she does not need to be told (or, worse, coerced) to learn; rather, she will find pleasure in the process, which is motivation to seek to learn more.

How to Use This Book

In this book, I have tried to share some of what I learned from the hundreds of children I taught and from parenting my son, now an adult. Children continue to be denied the education they could have, in favor of schooling, even in preschool. My own child came home from Kindergarten one day in tears. After he calmed and could talk, he articulated his fear, "Mommy, Kindergarten is taking away my imagination!" I realized then that I would have to be sure he could stay in touch with his imagination at home.

Every child has the right to express his imagination. The philosophy and ideas in this book are not for just some children, not for just children of means, not even just for typically developing children. Because you, as the adult, are providing materials and invitations and then moving forward according to your child's response to those materials and invitations, this is for every young child.

Each section of the book describes materials and ideas that will help you, as a parent, set up an environment for learning for your child. By "environment," I mean not only physical materials and experiences, but also an emotional environment, one in which your interaction with your child has an important role in your child's learning with her imagination intact. Embedded in the ideas in the book are opportunities to foster positive dispositions toward learning and habits of mind. You will find food for thought, lists of materials, and specific invitations. You may be tempted to jump to the invitations, but I suggest you first read what comes before. Everything hinges on your perspective and on, as we who are inspired by the schools of Reggio Emilia say, your image of the child.

Most of the materials in this book are either found/recycled, available in thrift shops like Goodwill, or are inexpensive craft store materials. You will find resources if you want to buy more expensive open-ended materials, but many of those can be replicated with supplies from home improvement or craft stores.

One of the joys I experienced when teaching young children was the transformation I saw in parents when they learned to see their children in a new light, a light that comes from joining their children in inquiry, from listening to them with their hearts and minds, and from expecting their children's thinking to amaze them. My hope is that this book will help parents make that connection with their children and that you will see your child with different eyes and be able to help him feed his hunger to learn, imagine, and create at home.

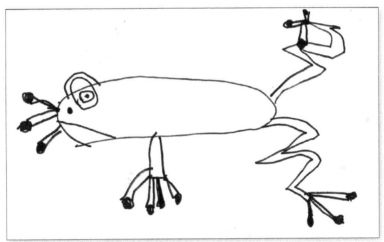

"Stand aside for a while and leave room for learning, observe carefully what children do, and then, if you have understood well, perhaps teaching will be different from before."

- Loris Malaguzzi

2 A Window Into Your Child's World

The Reggio Emilia Philosophy of Education

Reggio Emilia, a city in the northern part of Italy, is home to a world-class system of public infant-toddler centers and preschools (with growth toward post-primary education in recent years). The Reggio Emilia Approach is a philosophy based on a set of values about children and learning. Here is a quick primer on the tenets of the philosophy.

The image of the child. All children are seen as intelligent, competent, resourceful, and strong (as opposed to needy or as blank slates). Therefore, the child is respected and heard.

The environment. All that the child encounters in the learning context- places, things, and interactions- hold great possibilities for learning. The idea is that adults should plan for that learning by intentionally preparing the environment to be provocative, amiable, and beautiful. The environment is considered to be "the third teacher."

Relationship. We all learn best while in relationship with others. For the child, this includes relationships with peers and with adults. In addition, the child is driven to have a relationship with ideas and with the world around her. Collaboration among children, between adults and children, and between home and school is central to the work. Parents play a big role in the education of their children in the schools of Reggio Emilia.

Research. Emphasis on intellectual growth (and not academic proficiency alone) leads teachers to value and support children's research into big ideas that interest them and that the teachers believe hold value for the children. Likewise, the teachers are considered researchers of the children and how they learn, and of the learning process in general. Part of that research (for both children and adults) is documentation.

Documentation. Teachers create learning stories with photographs, artifacts, narrative, children's words, interpretation, and more, for the sake of children's and teachers' research, and to further learning for all.

The 100 Languages. One of the best ways for children to learn is by representing their thinking (what they understand and what they are trying to understand) symbolically, by drawing, painting, sculpting, constructing, making music, moving, and acting. When a child uses a medium to communicate, express, or figure things out, he is using the medium (or media!) as a language. In my experience, this is the richest ground for learning for young children.

I encountered the Reggio Emilia philosophy in 1990 and, as it resonated with my own philosophy of education, I began to both study the approach and bring it into my Junior Kindergarten classroom that year. I taught Kindergarten for eleven years before that, and I remember being amazed at how much more the children learned in Junior Kindergarten than they had in Kindergarten after I stopped trying to dictate exactly what the children would learn and when and started listening to them, trying to understand what and how they were thinking, and supporting their learning from there. I remember thinking that the images of children's representation (drawing, painting, clay sculptures) I saw from Reggio Emilia were impossible; no five-year-old could have done that! And then I began to support children's representation with many different media in my own classroom. Indeed, they can do "that!"

Observational drawing of a bicycle by a five-year-old child

In addition to making greater intellectual and academic progress, the children in the Reggio-inspired classroom developed personal resources beyond what I'd ever seen before. They came to know what fed their intellects (individually) and came to know and use each other's passions as inspiration for research. They became able to solve problems collaboratively, think of a plan B when plan A failed, have cognitive conflict without emotional conflict, and advocate for themselves and others.

Once, during tornado season, we were told in advance that we'd have a tornado drill at a specific time. At the appointed moment, we all gathered in the front entryway of our little house to wait out the drill. Suddenly, the front door opened, a security guard stuck an air horn into the entryway, and, not knowing we were already in place, let out a startling blast. We were all taken aback, and some of the children cried. For hours the children talked about it: how wrong it was for someone to frighten them like that and make them cry. They wanted to make sure it never happened again. Recognizing the children's need to *do* something with their outrage, I called a meeting so that they could discuss a course of action. I had thought they might want to write a letter to the security guard, but they thought it better to find the "boss" of security, state their case in person, and request that it never happen again. Four children—three who had cried and one who joined the group in support of her friends—volunteered to go. We found the head of security, and the children articulated their thoughts and feelings to him. At first, he tried to explain to them why he felt a blast into the building was necessary, but the children were having none of it. They insisted that he negotiate with them. In the end, he did, and they agreed that the next time there had to be a tornado drill a security guard would blast the air horn *outside* of the front door and certainly not inside without looking to see where the children were.

Part of what enabled the children to advocate for themselves is that each had found and knew how to use her voice. Since day one at school, teachers had listened when children talked. They expected children to listen to and respond to each other. The children had become accustomed to articulating their thinking and emotions. They were used to making choices (you'd be surprised how few preschoolers actually are), within limits that they understood and agreements that they made collectively for the good of everyone in the group.

"I Know How It Rains:" Listening in a New Way

Often when your preschooler asks a "how the world works" type question, he is really saying, "I have a theory. Ask me about it," or "Let's have a conversation about it." Yet, when adults hear "how the world works" questions, they tend to respond with an answer right away. Though there certainly are times we want to answer children's questions, it would be a pity to miss the relationship- and intellect-building conversations that happen when, instead of "the" answer, we ask a preschooler what *he* thinks. If you do this, you just might be amazed at the power of your child's thinking.

If your child asks you a question, you have a decision to make: Is it a question that might be fertile ground for conversation? Might your child really be asking you to talk with her about a theory she is developing? Or is she asking you what is for dinner? If it's the latter, by all means, go ahead and answer it. "When is my birthday?" is a question that requires an answer. But, "Where does the moon go in the day?" or "How does grandma get in the iPad when she FaceTimes me?" is an invitation to listen. You can ask, "What do you think?" or "What is your theory?" And then, when your child tells you what she thinks, continue to ask questions to clarify or gently challenge or expand her thinking. By doing this you are sending the message that you value her ideas (which will encourage future musings) and helping her develop skills of inquiry and communication.

Here's an example of the way a conversation about how things work might go. This is dialogue between a small group of children and a teacher (T), but a parent could listen and respond to one child in a similar way.

A child exclaimed, "I can hear the wind!"

We listened a bit, and then the teacher asked, "What is wind?"

Lydia: When you're blowing, like this (Lydia blows).

Julianna: It's air that's really strong.

Lydia: It carries away the leaves.

Mary: It's like kites, and when it carries away the leaves they go back up to the trees. T: They go back on the trees?

Lydia: Uh-uh. In Summer the leaves grow back, because in the trees they have little sprout things.

T: You don't think the leaves go back onto the trees?

Lydia: No. Because they're not magnets.

Lillie: When it's Fall, the wind is out the most, so when the wind blows as hard as he can, the leaves aren't strong enough to stay on the tree, so they go to the ground. And when it's Winter time they stay on the ground, but when it becomes Spring, they turn back green, and the wind blows them, and then they stick back onto the trees.

T: So we have two different theories, don't we? Why does that theory make sense to you, Lillie?

Lillie: Because when it becomes Winter the snow comes down and it comes all the way down and it cover-ups the leaves, and then the snow melts. The leaves don't become back on the ground any more. When you want to see the leaves when it's the end of Winter, you can't see them, because they're already back up on the tree.

T: So Lillie says that the reason that theory makes sense to her is because the leaves are gone. They're not on the ground any more.

Eleanor: Uh-uh. They're not. In the Winter, there's evergreen trees that leaves stay on.

T: So I wonder, when you go to the Outdoor Classroom today, what might you be seeing?

Lillie: Wind!

T: Can you see the wind?

Emmie: Feel the wind!

Lillie: It's clear!

Lauren: It goes round and round.

Lillie: No. The wind looks like nothing. It's clear.

Everyone at once (this is excitement): It's clear! The wind goes down!

Lillie: When it blows across the whole sky, there's no real clouds that are making it blow. There's a cloud up in the sky...a wind cloud up in the sky. The wind blows down, and then you can't see it, because the air comes down from the clouds, and the clouds are just like the air, and the air's the same color as clear.

T: But wait a minute. Can't we see the clouds?

Lillie: Yeah...

T: You said the wind is the same color as the clouds.

Lydia: That's why they blend in with each other.

T: So can you see wind or not, Lydia?

Lydia: They're both clear. You cannot see the clouds. Only in Summer.

Lillie: That's what I was saying.

Lydia: Right now it's so windy that you can't even see the clouds.

Mary: I can see the clouds, but I can't see the sky.

Julianna: I can see the clouds, but I can't see the sky. But I can't see the wind.

Lillie: I barely could see the clouds, because the clouds are the ones that are covering up the whole sky.

Seeing the World Through Your Child's Eyes

Have you ever gone down on your knees and looked at a space from your child's perspective? Try it, when no one's watching, or better yet, get someone to do it with you. Now imagine that everything you see is completely new to you. Put aside your adult worries and understandings and try to put on a lens of wonder. How do you see that spider web? As something to brush away to keep the fence looking clean? Or as a miraculous work of art? How do you see the dew on the grass: as an annoyance that will leave your shoes wet, or as the world gone sparkly? Your child is in touch with his imagination in a way many adults no longer are. To him, there are fairies in the woods and a tree can be a friend. Imagination, creativity, and invention are part of his everyday affairs. To think in this way is exciting and renewing, and it is not for children only. You can join your child in his magical world. In fact, if you do, you will be fostering his intellect and helping him grow his personal resources. This is an invitation into your child's world. It's an opportunity to ditch schooling in favor of education. And to rediscover magic for yourself.

Inviting your child to take photographs of what interests her on a nature walk will give you a window into her way of seeing the world.

Inviting Your Child to Represent His Ideas

What is representation, and why does it matter? When we represent an idea or experience, we are remaking it in some way, either physically or mentally. We must represent an idea in some way in order to really learn it (rather than just parrot back what we have heard, which I do not consider "learning," unless it is learning to give the adult in authority what she wants.) As an adult, I might hear a new idea and, if I'm motivated to make that idea part of my intellectual schema (i.e., learn), I will remake that idea either mentally or by writing it down or by talking to someone about it. The same process applies if we want to solve problems; we must represent the problem and possibilities in some way, externally or internally, in order to invent a solution. As adults, when we are faced with a difficult problem, we might talk it through, do some research (reading), write down pros and cons or take notes, and so forth. These are not languages in which young children are fluent, yet they are capable of thinking about big and important ideas. They just need the languages through which to express, communicate, invent, and figure things out. The languages accessible to young children are verbal language, modes of expression like drawing, painting, or constructing, for example, and temporal languages like movement, roleplay, or music.

Children need access to materials, time to learn how they work, and the disposition to represent their ideas. When he was four, my son (who is now, in his mid-twenties, a working artist) did not choose to draw much. Nor was he interested in writing his name, despite the fact that he had all the lovely materials and encouragement he might need to do both, and despite the fact that many four-year-olds know how to write their names. He was a nature kid. He loved animals and spending time outdoors. One day he saw a large, green Luna moth on a tree under which he was playing. He came running inside and yelled, "Quick, Mommy, we have to get the camera!" He wanted to capture the image of this lovely moth. But we discovered the camera needed to be charged (it was in the old days, before smartphone cameras). His face fell. "You could draw it so you can remember it," I suggested, not really thinking that he would accept the suggestion. But he agreed and, drawing from life, created the most amazing likeness of the moth (for a non-drawing four-year-old) in the tree! I learned some things from Tristan that day. For him, it was only worth drawing or playing on the violin or writing about if it was important and personal. Capturing the Luna moth for posterity was important and personal. The disposition (and inspiration) to draw and write had been his missing link.

It is moments like these that teach us the difference between schooling and education. Your child has all the personal equipment needed for his intellectual development. If we adults will observe, listen, learn from our children what lights their fire, enable our children's intent to learn, and offer challenges from there, we will be doing far more for their intellectual, personal, and academic growth than we could ever do with worksheets or flashcards.

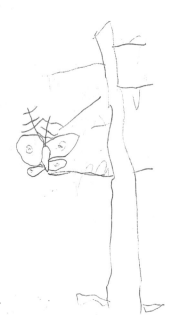

Tristan's Luna Moth

"Children — for the ways in which we have encountered them — are the first great researchers. If we are capable of listening to them, children can give us back our pleasure in wonder, in marveling, in doubt. Children can convey the joy of search and research which belongs not only to children, but to women, to men, to humankind: it belongs to life."

- Carla Rinaldi

3 Understanding your Child's World

Stages of Representation

Children begin to represent reality symbolically from an early age. They may feed a baby doll or pretend to fix a "broken" truck. Social media is full of videos of babies pretending to conduct an orchestra or dancing along to a televised Swan Lake. All of this we might call representation at the "body level." Older children also represent at the body level when they engage in dramatic play, pretending to be pirates chasing each other around the yard or constructing "stories" in their pretend family play ("Pretend I'm the mommy and you're the baby and you got sick and I had to take you to the doctor and…").

Sometime after her first year, a child will begin to represent symbolically with objects, pretending a block is a cell phone, for example, or driving her carrot around her highchair saying, "Vroom vroom." She is making the block or the carrot stand in for, or represent, the real object. This is her thinking getting just a little bit more abstract. When she gets a bit older, she will play pretend with models (dinosaurs, animals, dollhouse figures, and Playmobil sets, for example). Let's call this playing at the "toy level." Toy level play is one type of symbolic representation. In time, children begin to engage in more sophisticated symbolic representation by drawing, painting, sculpting, and constructing.

Each successive level of representation is another step away from the actual object that is being represented. That is, a block stands in for a cellphone, but a drawing of a cell phone is a more abstract, and therefore mature, representation of the cell phone.

The third level of representation is the sign level: writing. Writing "cellphone" is yet more abstract—further removed from the actual cell phone—than the drawing of a cell phone.

Although these stages of representation happen developmentally—that is, a toddler can represent the cellphone with a block but cannot write the word "cellphone"—these behaviors do not necessarily go away with maturity. Rather, the 6-year-old may be able to write "cellphone," and writing might be the most satisfactory type of representation to him at the time, but he might also sometimes draw a cellphone or pretend to be talking on one.

Levels of Representation

Body Level ► Symbolic Level: Toy ► Symbolic Level: Graphic ► Sign Level (writing)

What parents can do to support children's desire to represent in increasingly abstract ways is to recognize what satisfies the child at the moment and be ready to provide support and materials that will be more satisfying as she grows. So, say one day you observe your toddler talking for her toy elephant. She is giving you a window into her ability to represent and a clue for the kinds of materials you can provide. Be ready for her, with people and animal models, as well as little cars and maybe some blocks or boxes for making houses or caves. All you need do is put the materials where she can access them. And enjoy watching her represent what she knows and imagines. You will, of course, want to be mindful of the age of your child and the size of the toys as potential choking hazards.

Or say you have given your three-year-old glue and access to recyclables. She has been gluing with abandon, apparently consumed with the process of it all. Then, one day, she declares intent to make a house with the same materials. Again, she's given you a window into her development. She wants to use those materials to represent something specific. Now she may need support she didn't earlier. Perhaps she needs you to cut a door in the cardboard or help her find clear plastic for windows. Or perhaps her workspace needs to change, because she needs to leave her work supplies out longer or she needs a strong base on which to build. And perhaps she needs tips and techniques or emotional support she didn't need before. You want to have the material and emotional flexibility to walk alongside your child as she grows. This is education.

The Development of Drawing

A toddler may not have intent to represent any particular object through drawing. But she should have a chance to explore many different media for drawing so that when she is ready to represent an idea or object she will have all the personal tools necessary to do so. Give your toddler non-toxic drawing media that make dark, satisfying marks. She'll probably go through a lot of paper. The toddler draws with gesture: large arm movements, usually without intent to represent anything in particular. She delights in the marks she can make, and her engagement is primarily in the relationship between her movements and the marks on the paper. She will draw lines and circles and scribbles. She will not likely change colors with intention, though she might experiment to see if all of the markers behave the same. She should have access to big paper with a variety of textures and a variety of tools: crayons, markers, pencils, chalk. She will go through a lot of paper.

As the toddler grows, perhaps at age 3, she develops a desire to represent. She may scribble and then "name" the scribble (This is Daddy mowing the lawn). In time, she will have intent as she is scribbling and say, "I'm drawing Daddy mowing the lawn." You can engage her in conversation about her drawing. You might ask, "What's happening now?" She may engage in "mapping," that is, marking an event with a scribble or shape in a space on the paper, not really drawing any recognizable forms. Even when she does start drawing figures, she may continue to place them around the paper in a more event-based way than in any kind of visual relationship.

In the examples below, Tristan, at age 3 and a half, shows in a series of drawings done on one day that he is in transition from scribbling to representational drawing.

There's the volcano (left). This is another volcano, erupting (while "erupting" vigorously as he drew).

An early human figure: That's my friend who's McKenzie.

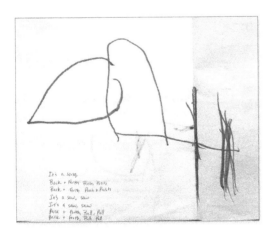

Tristan, age 3 and a half, gave meaning to the motions of his drawing, turning it into a song.

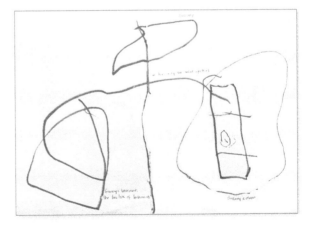

An example of mapping. Here Tristan mapped a story of his Granny's movements: Top: Granny. Lower left: Granny's basement. She has lots of basements. Top: The way she went upstairs. Bottom right: Granny's door.

In time, your child will declare intent to draw something before he draws. As he grows, your child will put figures in visual relationship to each other in his drawings, and he will begin to consider perspective. He will "ground" his figures, placing them on a baseline he has drawn or at the very bottom of the page. He will make Daddy taller than himself. He will put the sun in the sky and the tree on the ground. Depending on how much experience with materials for drawing a child has had, this could occur anywhere from age 4 to 5 ½.

An example of grounding in a 5-year-old's drawing, with perspective

You may notice that your preschool/primary school-aged child seems to draw the same objects over and over and over. He may be engaging in what I call "formula" drawing. Having developed a repertoire of things he knows how to draw, that's what he draws. That's all he draws. As he develops greater fluency, he will begin to add new elements to his formula drawings (i.e. his usual tree, house, and birds, but also a novel zebra). In time, he will have the facility and confidence to draw whatever he is thinking about and to use drawing as a language.

If you are observing your child's growth in drawing, you will notice that, once he is using drawing as a language (to communicate, express, and figure things out), he will draw for different purposes.

- He may draw to explain what he's thinking.
- He may draw his imagination.

- He may draw to practice particular figures.
- He may draw to represent something that really happened to him.
- He may draw to figure out how something works.
- He may draw to tell a story.

This is not a comprehensive list. In what other ways does your child use drawing to learn? Becoming attuned to the purposes your child finds for drawing will make the process more fun for you and will help you foster your child's growth, not just in drawing, but in the ways that drawing supports thinking, emotional regulation, and even learning to read and write.

Tools For Drawing

Your child should be able to use a tool that will best help her draw what she is thinking. That is, the child who wants to draw with detail will struggle to do so with fat markers. The child who wants to color a large area will struggle with a fine-line pen. You want to think developmentally, too. The toddler may be drawing with gestures, rather than with intent to draw anything in particular. What would be most satisfying for her? Perhaps thick washable markers? Put yourself back into a state of seeing the world through your child's eyes and offer what you think would help her realize her intent.

Science and Magical Thinking

Young children engage in magical thinking. Often that magical thinking includes external powers like God or Santa Claus or superheroes as agents of the unknown. For example, in one conversation in Junior Kindergarten, the children tackled the question, "How does the sun appear in the day and disappear at night?" Some children thought God lifted up the sun in the day.

"I think God lifts it up because he's very powerful. Yeah, because he can lift it up, because he can hold up the whole wide world."

We can't see God do this, they said, "Because he's outside the world."

"And the sun is outside the world."

"God puts invisible stuffing on his hands so people cannot see his hands lifting up the sun."

"How could the sun get to Richmond in time when it's morning?"

"It goes really, really fast to the other side of the earth. And then it keeps trading places with the moon."

Enjoy your child's magical thinking. In time, magical theories will no longer make sense to him, and he will begin to feel dissatisfied with them. Logic and experience will start to influence his thinking. You will notice this shift toward more scientific thinking if you are listening and if your child feels comfortable posing his theories from an early age. That comfort level comes with your invitations to your child to tell you what he thinks and with your resistance to the urge to tell your child what *you* know about what he's wondering. Listen, ask clarifying questions, challenge his thinking. In general, if your child remains engaged with the conversation, you'll know you haven't taken over the thought process. If what you say ends the conversation, you'll know you've said too much.

At around seven years old, children seem to become more interested in "facts." Magical thinking may no longer be satisfying to them, and they begin to want "real answers." Children's research then takes on another quality. If your child has engaged in active construction of theory from a young age, he will know how to continue his research in his more fact-oriented state.

Documenting Your Child's Learning

Every child in my class had a personal portfolio that told the story of her learning during that year. In it were:

- Photographs of her drawings and other representation
- Her insightful thoughts in quotes we wanted to remember
- Photographs of her working on collaborative projects
- Videos of plays the children wrote and in which she participated

You can do this at home as well. In addition to the kinds of pages we included at school, you can add:

- Documentation of milestones: the first drawing that your child names; his first sleep in a big-boy bed; her first writing, etc.
- Videos of important moments. You can do this by:
  - uploading a video from a smartphone to Youtube, Vimeo, or another video service
  - uploading the url for the video that the video service gives you to a qr code creator and printing out the qr code for the portfolio.
  - scanning the qr code with a cellphone app to see the video
- Anything else that represents her learning story

The portfolio itself can be a simple three-ring binder. We were able to keep traces of big or three-dimensional pieces by photographing them, printing the photos out, dating them, and inserting them chronologically into the notebook. This works for items that can't go into the portfolio for any reason. The teachers used these portfolios for authentic assessment purposes and to show parents what we were learning about their children. The children used the portfolios for a very different purpose. They often pulled them out and sat with them, poring over the pages, as a way to revisit themselves in an earlier state. They often did this in pairs, commenting, "I remember when I used to draw like that!" or reminiscing about a favorite shared moment. When we had visitors, out came the portfolios, and the children would invite the visitors to sit and look at their portfolios with them. The children recognized and cherished their portfolios as the story of themselves. Parents tell me that, decades later, they still have their child's Junior Kindergarten portfolio and revisit it fondly.

The benefits to keeping a portfolio at home, especially if your child doesn't have one at school, are many. It allows for:

- Giving your child the opportunity to revisit her own thinking, process, and growth

- The creation of a learning story, which may help your child develop a sense of herself as a student

- Encouraging reflection. If your child's best efforts go into her portfolio and she gets a voice in choosing, she may begin to think about her work in a more reflective way.

- An opportunity for you to see your child's growth in a concrete way

- A keepsake of a time that is fleeting and precious, increasingly so as your child grows up

Two children look at their portfolios beside each other

If you decide to create a portfolio for your child, you can create one for each year. On her birthday, you can review the previous year's portfolio and present her with a new one as part of your child's birthday celebration. Or you can create one portfolio for preschool and one for the primary grades. Either way, your child's learning story should be honored and celebrated.

"Our task is to help children communicate with the world using all their potential, strengths, and languages, and to overcome any obstacle presented by our culture."

- Loris Malaguzzi

4 Expanding Your Child's World

Invitations for Engagement

Educators in Reggio Emilia call certain invitations for engagement "provocations." They might be questions or naturally occurring events (a mysterious rainbow cast on a playroom wall, for example), or they might be new and intriguing materials placed in the environment. You can offer materials as provocations that you think your child might enjoy by simply placing them where he will find them. Then watch and see what he does with them. For example, when your child wakes up from his nap, he finds flowers from the garden, a magnifying glass, and drawing materials on the playroom table. Or strips of paper and tape. Or old CDs and colored Sharpie pens. Your interaction with him starts with what he does with the provocation; observe and follow your child's lead from there. You can invite your child to articulate his plan, perhaps, or narrate his process as he explores. Listen. Ask yourself, "What's my child's perspective?" and "What's being learned here?" You can invite him to go deeper into his process when he thinks he's finished ("What else do you see on that flower?" for example, or "What else can you do with _____?"). You can invite him to record the results of his research if that's appropriate ("Would you like me to write your words about it in your journal?").

Provocations are a starting place, and you don't always have to be the one to provide them. They may simply appear, like the rainbow, or your child may discover them on her own. Over time you may have to provide them less and less as your child develops an awake mind that expects to follow curiosity, and she seeks out provocations on her own. Whatever the source of a provocation, you will want to be careful not to impose a particular agenda as you offer a provocation. This is not "sneak teaching." The exchange between adult and child around a provocation begins with the child. The adult's job is to try to figure out the child's intent—what is she trying to figure out?—so that you can support her in that effort. As a teacher, I was often amazed at how much more complex or creative or symbolic children's thinking was when I didn't try to assume what they would take away from a particular provocation.

At school, we did not offer a new provocation every day. Rather, we tried to offer provocations that we thought the children would find interesting and left them out until the children no longer were engaging with them.

Natural materials and a magnifying glass combine to make provocation for seeing the familiar in a new way.

The Difference Between Provocations and Activities

I define an activity as something an adult has provided that carries a specific expectation of how it will be executed. For example, a set of materials that requires the child to match like objects would be an activity. A game with rules would be an activity. A worksheet might be an activity. An activity is usually closed-ended, and usually has a limited draw for a child's engagement. Many children's toys are activities, which is why you might see longer and deeper engagement with the box than with the toy! There is nothing inherently wrong with activities. Puzzles are closed-ended (there is one solution to the puzzle), and they can be both enjoyable and educational. The same for games with rules and many educational toys. But you don't need to hear about those. They are ubiquitous in every toy store and, probably, populated your own childhood.

Provocations, on the other hand, are invitations to explore. They might be questions or materials that make the mind go, "What??!!" or that call the mind toward them. A provocation might be something surprising or just something that piques curiosity. A provocation that "works" is one that engages the child for an extended period of time and/or can take the child in many different directions. Not all provocations that you offer will be successful. This is because whether a provocation speaks to a child depends on both what interests her at the moment and what she is ready to undertake. Whether something you offer a child "takes" or not, observing your child's response to a provocation leaves you wiser about your child at the moment and may lead you to what might be more interesting to her.

The One Hundred Languages of Children

The educators of Reggio Emilia describe the means of expression available to children as "100 languages." Of course, no one has counted the languages of learning for young children. "One hundred" is a metaphor for the plethora of possibilities for expression of which children are capable. I have seen children do impressive things with paper clips, for example, and I don't think they are on anyone's list of languages. When you shift your thinking from educational toys to materials for exploration and representation, you expand the possibilities for learning beyond what adults, with our relatively dormant imaginations, can "assign."

Why Materials Matter

No five-year-old, no matter how loquacious, can do justice to her biggest ideas verbally. Children are capable of profound thinking. Given a chance, your young child will take on questions of philosophy, theology, systems, mathematical relationships, science, and more. She just isn't likely to have the verbal language yet to represent those ideas fully (and therefore to think further about them). But she can represent big ideas through visual and temporal languages, i.e. drawing, painting, sculpting, constructing, acting, and so on. Her visual representation supports her verbal language, her verbal language supports her graphic language. That reciprocity supports your child's overall growth in big ways.

The youngest children need to learn what materials will do and what they will let them do, and they need to learn the skills involved in manipulating materials. If he does, by the time a child has a desire to represent, the facility with media is there. So, what do you need so that your child can explore materials and later use them to represent his biggest ideas? The suggestions in the following sections should be considered *possibilities*. You wouldn't want to offer everything all at once, but offer one set of materials, watch what your child does with them, and when you think he could use a new challenge, offer another. You can also offer a different combination of materials as a new challenge. Good quality materials are more satisfying to use than cheaper quality materials. For example, it can be much less satisfying to draw with markers on newsprint than on smooth white paper. Here's where your imagination dances with the child's imagination.

You might think that you need to set up a homeschool classroom for your preschool or primary school-aged child. Certainly, it helps to have a table and chairs for him to use. You will want an area that can be cleared for big projects. Even better if the projects can be left out for continued work and play for a few days. Beyond that, what's needed are *materials, time,* and *a listening adult.*

Exploration

Whatever the materials, children need to have many experiences with a medium before they are likely to represent with it. When we introduced clay in Junior Kindergarten, for example, we set the expectation that the children explore first. It was often a new medium for the children, and they would pound, pinch, poke, break, and join joyfully, sometimes over many sittings, before they ever declared intent to "make" something. That exploratory experience with media is important if your child is to learn what a medium will do and will let him do. Let making things come in its own time.

Drawing Every Day

I believe that children should draw every day. Why drawing?

Drawing is, in my opinion, one of the most important symbolic languages for your child to develop. The reasons are many.

- The materials for drawing are almost always available (unlike clay for sculpting, for example).
- Drawing helps us see the familiar in a new way. In fact, it is said that you never *really* see something until you have tried to draw it.
- Drawing is "rehearsal" for writing; it prepares the mind for learning to write, including practice in the all-important task of accessing ideas and getting them out on paper.
- Drawing can help a child communicate when words won't suffice.
- Drawing can be supremely satisfying, both as expression and as communication.

It's a great endeavor to suggest when you are busy in the kitchen, while you are working from home, or during "quiet time" before bed. Paper and tools for drawing should be stored where the child can access them easily, if possible.

Responding to Your Child's Work: "What's Happening Here?"

When your child shows you a drawing, painting, or something she has made, your response can make a big difference in how she feels about herself and her work. If your toddler does not yet talk, you can respond to what your child is showing you is important to her. While she is drawing or painting, you can comment on her process. "Oh, now you are making BIG circles!" or "You are covering the whole paper!" But if she is older and has intention to represent in her drawing, try asking, "What's happening here?" This elicits conversation. If your child tells you "It's Fido and me. We're taking a walk," you can encourage her to talk more by asking, "Oh! Where are you going?"

The more she talks about her drawing, the more she engages with it, and she might even say, "Oh! I forgot to draw the park!" and return to her drawing. In this way, the drawing supports language and language supports drawing.

Perhaps your child doesn't have "something happening" in her drawings yet. Then she may respond to your question with *her* idea of what is happening in the picture, such as "*all* the colors" or "A big ball." Just by asking the question and engaging her in conversation, you are inviting her to grow in her representation.

Taking Story Dictation

Once your child is telling you "what's happening" in his drawings, you can ask him if he'd like you to write his words about his picture, either beside the picture or on a card to go with the picture (let him choose). Say the words as you print what your child dictates about his picture. Try not to rephrase his words, but write what he says as he says it. Then, if you save his stories, you will have documentation of his growth as his language matures, something you can enjoy years later. If you are concerned about his syntax or that his story doesn't make sense, try reading his words back to him. He may say, "Hey! That doesn't make sense!" and choose to revise his story. If he doesn't notice anything off, don't worry. As long as you continue to write his stories for him, another opportunity will come. If he does notice his story doesn't make sense and wants to change it, what a great way to learn about revision in the writing process! Writing your child's stories for him lets him see that his words, when they are written, can become permanent (where they otherwise are temporal, disappearing into air as he says them)— a way to keep his words. This is an important literacy concept. In time, your child's stories may become longer, more structured, and/or more cohesive.

Troubleshooting

Once your child, perhaps at age 4, has a desire to draw figures and under-stands that others can draw what they are thinking, you may see some frus-tration emerge. She may ask you to draw for her, declare intent to draw some-thing but call it something else when it doesn't look like her mental image of it, crumple up her drawing in frustration, or simply give up. You can help here. Tell her, "I won't draw it for you, but I will help you do it." Then talk her through.

Let's say your child wants to draw a dog. Ask, "What does a dog have?" If she says, "A tail," and you know that's a hard place from which to start, say, "And what else?" A head or a body is a good place to start, so when she offers one of those, say "What shape is it?" or "What does it look like?" If she doesn't know how to draw the shape she identifies, you can help her practice the shape, even holding her hand if necessary. Try to remember that your goal is to allow your child to realize her intent by herself as much as possible. Her satisfaction trumps yours. If she is satisfied with a circle she has drawn but you aren't, let it be, no matter how difficult that may be. This is her dog! If she is not satisfied, you can lend her your patience and confidence that she can do it as she tries again. If she does not know what a dog has, on the other hand, she may not have a complete enough mental image of "dog" to draw one. This can happen even if she is intimately familiar with dogs. In this case, you would want to look at a picture of a dog together and talk about the parts and shapes you see.

What if her big brother says to your young child, "THAT doesn't look like a dog!"? Rather than chastise the brother, you might try inviting the little one to ask her brother to help her make her dog look more like a dog. That puts the brother into a different, more helpful, state of power, and gives the little sister his helpful attention, a win for both. If the brother complains, "She's copying me!" try helping him see that his little sister admires his competence and wants to learn from him. In my Junior Kindergarten classes, we would often invite children to check in with other children when they thought they were finished with a drawing, painting, or sculpture and ask, "What else does my _____ need?" That created a culture in which children sought other children out for support, recognized each other's expertise, and were willing to learn from each other.

Opportunities for Drawing

On his own, given materials and time, your child will draw in order to practice forms (learning to draw people, for example), express imagination, tell stories, explore design, communicate a message, and so on. But you can offer invitations for drawing that your older child might not think of on his own.

- Contour Drawing (or painting). When engaging in contour drawing, the drawer follows the edge of an object, such as a leaf, with a finger and, without picking up the pen, tries to follow the movement of the non-dominant hand with the pen or brush.

- Keeping a journal. Preschoolers and primary school-aged children often enjoy having a journal of their very own, a book of their thoughts, experiences, and ideas. For children to appreciate the power of a journal, adults often have to facilitate its use, as often children's first impulse is to scribble on each page quickly to just fill the space. The journal can be useful as a tool you bring out when your child wants to record an experience for posterity through drawing and then put in a safe place for the next opportunity.

- Making books. You can make a simple blank book by stapling pages together, but there are other clever ways to make blank books in which your child can draw and write.

Here are directions for making a simple fold-and-cut 8-page tiny book:

Fold a piece of letter-sized paper in half.

Fold it again the other way.

Fold it again.

Open it to the half fold.

Hold the paper so the long side is facing you. You will see the fold lines in a cross. Cut through both layers on the fold line in the middle and only to the intersecting fold line.

Open all the way and fold the opposite way you had it when you cut. It should look like a "hot dog" (as opposed to a "hamburger").

Push the two ends in toward each other. That will make the middle stick out. Keep pushing in until the two quarters on the outside touch.

Fold it all in half, and you have your book.

Here is a YouTube video link that might be easier to follow than written directions: https://www.youtube.com/watch?v=21qi9ZcQVto

If that was fun, here's a link to more ways to make books, some easy enough for young children to make, others more complicated: https://www.wiki-how.com/Make-a-Booklet-from-Paper

How to Make a Quick and Easy 8 Page Mini-Book From One Piece of Paper

3 Ways to Make a Booklet from Paper

A four-year-old uses a "thinking pen" to draw her self-portrait

• Drawing portraits. You can invite your child to draw a self-portrait of just her face. Provide a mirror, paper, and thinking pen (thin, black felt-tipped pen). Encourage your child to really draw what she sees. This is a great thing to do when something changes: your child loses a tooth, gets a haircut, gets braids in her hair for the first time, etc.

• Drawing motion. What does someone look like when they are dancing? Running? Sleeping? A full- length mirror might help here. Or take photographs of your child in action and let her use the images as referents as she is drawing.

• Drawing emotion. What does a face look like when the person is sad? Worried? Surprised? Provide a mirror and encourage your child to draw more detail than just the position of the mouth.

• Drawing perspective. What does the dog look like from the back? The side? What would the dog look like to an ant? To a giant? Use your imagination to think of more challenges.

Combining Media

Once children are proficient with media, combining them adds complexity and new interest. An example would be drawing outlines with permanent ink and adding color with pencils or watercolor; or drawing with sidewalk chalk on the driveway or on slates and then painting over the drawing with water.

Look for suggestions of other combinations in the sections that follow.

Paint the World

There's something immensely satisfying about painting, and variations abound! Combining one kind of paint with different surfaces and one kind of surface with different paints yield completely different experiences. Here are some ideas:

- Tempera (water-based) paint on butcher paper (great for infants and toddlers)

Tempera paint on a plexiglass panel. The panel replaced fence sections, giving the children a way to peek through to the other side. The light shining through the panel gave the paintings a luminescence that delighted everyone who saw them. Often we'd keep the murals for a few days, until rain washed them away, but if children wanted to make a new mural before nature erased the panel, we used water and a squeegee to prepare for a new opportunity.

- Tempera paint on corrugated cardboard
- Acrylic paint (more or less permanent), tempera paint or finger paint (washable) on plexiglass
- Water on a wooden fence or on slate
- Liquid watercolor on paper (vivid if you don't water it down)
- Liquid watercolor on shells or dried clay (muted, since the surface is porous)
- Acrylic paint on aluminum foil
- Acrylic paint on clean rocks
- Tempera paint on a large box
- Make your own natural paint brushes by attaching different textured plants/flowers to a stick with a rubber band. Best for painting on a large surface.
- Paint a mural on paper taped either on the floor or to a wall.
- Paint an entire picture with black outline only and go back to add color after the black paint dries.
- Mix 6 shades of one color with your child, letting him choose the degree of change to make with each iteration. Then he can paint with all the hues he has made.

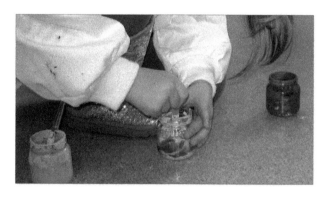

◄ *Painting with all the blue hues children have made*

- Paint with acrylic paint on a clear shower curtain, or part of one, to make a mural.

A mural of Fairy World painted collaboratively by five-year-olds. Acrylic paint on clear plastic shower curtain

- Invite your child to paint with liquid watercolors on coffee filters. The colors will bleed and make beautiful designs. If you hang the dried paintings in the window, the colors will seem to glow.
- Gather sticks with interesting shapes and paint them with acrylic or tempera paint. What can you make with the painted sticks? A mobile? A sculpture (use clay balls to stand sticks up)?

Painting sticks collected on a nature walk

- Invite your child to plan a city's roads for block building and car play.

  You need:

  ○ A large piece of cotton duck fabric

  ○ A pencil

  ○ Grey or black (and yellow or white if your child wants lines on the roads) acrylic paint.

Plan out the roads with your child. His age will determine how much help you will need to offer. In Junior Kindergarten, the children negotiated where they wanted the roads to go, and I drew with pencil what they told me to draw. I took the opportunity to challenge their thinking when a road seemed to go nowhere or a "place" they wanted to have in their city did not have an access road. Then they painted the roads. Later, they painted lines on the roads, made cardboard signs for it, constructed buildings out of cardstock and boxes, and built bridges. The piece remained an option for block area play for many years.

- Dilute liquid watercolor (a little paint to a lot of water; the amount will depend on what you want to paint and how intense you want your colors to be) in a few spray bottles. Invite your child to paint with the spray bottle:

  ○ On large paper, preferably outside, as this *will* get messy

  ○ On snow

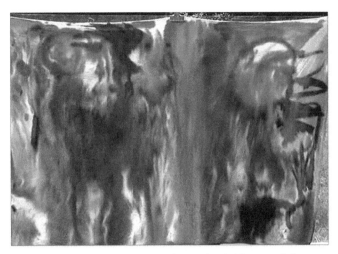

Liquid watercolor painted on a sheet. The children used this as a cubby house cover for many years

○ On a flat white sheet. You can use the sheet, once it is dried, as a fort or cubby house cover, or you can cut it into smaller pieces to use for dress-up (see section on Dress-up and Dramatic Play). This can be done with undiluted liquid watercolor and paintbrushes as well.

Offer your older child a variety of paintbrush sizes so that she can choose a brush that fits her purpose: tiny brushes for detail and diminutive marks, larger brushes for broad strokes and filling large spaces.

Dramatic Play

Roleplay is children's way of understanding the social and emotional world: What does it feel like to be a mommy or daddy? How does it feel to be big and in charge? Dramatic play also is a way of representing, and thereby managing, strong emotion: I am a fierce tiger and I can conquer anything that threatens me (and in doing so, keep myself safe)! It is supremely satisfying for children. They will engage in dramatic play whether or not you provide materials or particular opportunities for it, but there are things you can do to encourage growth in this kind of representation and things you can do to make it even more fun.

A group of preschool children played "lion chasing puppies" every day on the playground. The play was highly active and highly emotional. The teacher noticed that the children occasionally became overwhelmed by the emotion in the play, and they often complained that the lion did not listen when they screamed "Stop!" The teacher decided to call a meeting of the lion and puppies, to see if they could come to some agreement so that everyone felt safe in this play that they clearly wanted to continue. The puppies expressed frustration that the lion did not stop chasing them and roaring when they asked.

"But you were laughing, and you were running," the lion said. "I didn't know."

"How will you let the lion know you mean it when you say 'Stop!'?" the teacher asked.

After some discussion, the children agreed that they would put a hand out like a traffic cop when they said 'Stop' so that the lion would know that they were serious and that the lion would then stop.

"And sometimes I want to be the lion," someone declared.

So, the negotiation continued. They would take turns being the lion.

But the teacher was still concerned that this play did not seem to be growing. She understood that 'danger and safety' were big ideas for children (well, for all of us). Away from the playground, she initiated a conversation about danger, fear, and safety.

"What do you know about lions?" she asked the children.

What ensued was a series of conversations, drawings, and play that flowed from lions to monsters to vampires to robbers to hiding places to traps for bad guys to mechanisms for vanquishing danger. The teacher noticed the children's focus evolve from fear to courage and empowerment—expressed primarily in their dramatic play.

I tell this story to illustrate the power of dramatic play to enhance children's personal resources. Granted, if you are home alone with one child, she cannot engage in *social* dramatic play. But there is value in stretching one's identity in roleplay, even if alone.

Since one goal of teaching and learning in this way is that you will know your child better so you can support her growing into all she can be in an authentic way, try not to impose your idea of what your child should pretend to be. Rather, enjoy your window into her imagination and observe how her pretend play changes over time.

The Importance of Taking Risks and the Child's Right to Try

For a generation now, "safety" has been a primary concern in the creation of play spaces for children. But study after study has found that serious injuries in those "safe" play spaces *increased (Rosin 2014)*. Why? Because children are driven to test their abilities. They need to, in order to know what they can do, to know where their limits are and how and when to take risks safely. When safe play spaces do not offer challenges that allow them to test their capabilities, children tend to create those challenges by using equipment in unsafe ways, like climbing to the top of a swingset. When I designed an outdoor classroom, I had boulders installed at various heights, the tallest at 3 feet, in a large sand pit. The children saw them as a little bit dangerous to climb and jump off of. It took a *little* bit of courage to navigate those rocks, which made them deliciously inviting. No one ever got more than a skinned knee on those rocks, because the children saw them as a challenge and learned to pay attention when they were on them. Do you know where most of our bandaids went? To children who fell while running on our perfectly flat sidewalk or tripped over the four-inch-high boundary of the sand pit. They just weren't paying attention because, in their eyes, there were no challenges there.

I know parents who, as their children climb on rocks or walk on low walls, say repeatedly, "Be careful! Be careful!" What message is this sending to a child who is listening (many don't)? I don't trust that you will be safe. How will a child learn to trust his body and his judgment if he keeps getting a message that says, "You can't trust yourself"? I teach parents and teachers to say, instead (if they must), "Pay attention." That's often unnecessary, but is really what you want the child to be saying to himself. Do supervise. Do catch him if he falters and reassure him if he falls, and certainly stop him from climbing to the top of that swingset, as a fall from there could be truly dangerous. But if the worst that can happen is that a child gets a skinned knee, while the best is that he learns a little bit more about what his body can do at the moment, and what his courage will and will not let him do, then the best course of action is to let him try.

Similarly, parents and teachers often forbid children to play with sticks or rocks. But sticks and rocks have tremendous scope for the imagination! Instead of forbidding them, why not make an agreement, based on reason, as to what is OK to do with sticks and rocks and what is too dangerous? You and your child might agree that building with sticks or digging with sticks is safe, but running with them isn't. You might agree that you can do what you want with rocks as long as they don't fly through the air. Whatever the agreement, it should be a conversation rather than an edict, so that your child can begin to construct for herself the ability to make good decisions about risk-taking and safety.

Then there is the matter of tools. Children with big ideas need real tools to realize their intent. Sometimes those tools may be sharp or you may wonder if your child is old enough to handle grown-up tools. Again, preschoolers know when tools might be risky, and they tend to pay attention when using them. If you supervise, your four-year-old can use a paring knife to cut his fruit. He can use a sharp pencil if he knows how to keep himself safe with it. She can use a hammer if she knows how to use it safely. He can use a needle to sew. I have known children who really thought a needle intended to jump up and prick them, because they'd been taught that needles are not for children. Taking small risks and exercising her courage for the sake of making her idea visible puts your child in a growing place mentally and emotionally.

Dress-up

Most families have some sort of dress-up available for children. Here are some ideas to enhance your offerings:

- **Fabric as Flexible Dress-up**

Although you can certainly keep a trunk-full or set of hooks full of "real" dress-up clothes for your child, I always prefer simpler, more versatile options. Sheer cloth of different colors can be wrapped or clipped on the body to make nearly any costume desired, and it does double duty as a blanket, a river, a hiding place with visibility, a fort cover, emergency "wings," and much more. Add elastic headbands and wooden clothespins, and you have enormous scope for the imagination.

- **Fairy wings**

You can make wings for dress-up so easily! Fairy wings, bat wings, dragon wings, bird wings, any kind of wings your child needs to transform himself. All you need is one yard of sheer fabric and an elastic headband,

the kind that goes around a child's entire head. You might provide black fabric for bats, green for dragons, and so on. Tie the headband around the middle of the fabric. Both fabric and headband will look like two-dimensional bows. Then your child puts each arm through a loop and wears the wings like a backpack. You can sew or tie small hair ties or rubber bands on two corners of the wings for fingers to go through, or your child can just hold the ends in his hands. When he runs, his wings will flutter up like real wings.

- **Horse halter**

While observing children playing horse and rider or dog and walker, I noticed them trying to tie ropes around each other's necks. Not such a good idea! So, we made harnesses with lengths of 5/8" wide cotton webbing (the width isn't really that important). We sewed the ends of the webbing together to make a big circle. The horse puts the harness on like a backpack and the rider holds the other end of the loop. This makes a satisfying harness without putting anything around the neck.

- **Forts and Houses**

Growing up, my son always had a big box. Sometimes we transformed it into a house, sometimes into a puppet theater, sometimes a rocket ship. When one box became too tattered to stand, we would find another, and my son would decide what he wanted the new box to become. When he was old enough, he drew a design for the structure, and his dad or I wielded the box cutter. Sometimes we would collaborate with him on design problems (how to make the kind of roof he wanted, for example), but most of the time he directed the construction. He would furnish the structure on the inside and decorate both inside and outside, sometimes with markers and sometimes with paint. When someone we knew bought a large appliance, we asked if we could have the box (no one ever said no!)

and occasionally sought out boxes from appliance stores. You can also combine boxes to make structures with multiple rooms (or cars or anything your child imagines). A box can become so many things!

Scan the qr code for: Table Hammocks

Scan the qr code for: Made From A Cardboard Box

A table with four legs (as opposed to a pedestal table) can become a wonderful shelter as well. Just drape the table with a sheet or other cloth big enough to go to the floor on all sides (or three sides if you push the table against a wall). Furnish the shelter with pillows, stuffed animals, books, and a flashlight, and you have a lovely hideout.

You can also make a hammock with a four-legged table and fabric. Drape a long length of strong fabric (sheers won't do for this application) under the table and tie the ends on top of the table with multiple strong knots.

If you want something more permanent but extremely flexible, you can make a cubby house frame. The frame is made of four open wood panels, each made with 1x1s. Each panel is 4' by 4' and has a vertical cross piece in the middle and a horizontal piece in the middle of one side. When you assemble the four panels into a cube you create the frame of a house that children can drape with cloths or large paper decorated according to their imagination. At times, our cubby house also became a dark house (see the section on shadows), a puppet theater, and a frame for weaving (see the section on weaving). You can disassemble the cubby house for storage or use just two or three panels at a time. Use your imagination!

The four panels of the cubby attached in a way that creates a room divider.

The cubby house panels lashed together into a cube with cord and draped (by the children) with fabric and a transparent mural.

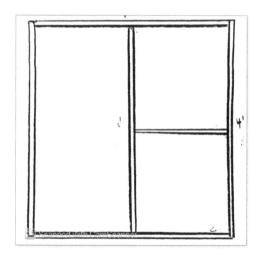

Here we have strung one of the "windows" of the cubby house with string, so the children could use it as a loom for weaving. The "roof" is simply a large piece of cloth draped over the edges of the cubby house and gathered to a point attached to a set of shelves above. The purple cloth and all other embellishments are the children's construction, attached with big wooden clips.

Construction

Though you might first conjure images of blocks or woodworking when you think of construction, I am defining it as the combining of like or unlike pieces of almost anything, often in a temporary way. In addition to blocks, recycled materials, sticks and stones, multiples of anything that can stand, paper, and traditional building toys can be materials for construction.

Blocks come in many forms, weights, and sizes. If you can afford unit blocks, they are great not only for building, but also for developing an understanding of mathematical relationships, since they are sized such that two squares ("halfs") equal one unit, two units equal one long block ("twos"), and two long blocks equal one "four block." See Appendix for a source for unit blocks.

However, you don't need unit blocks to encourage construction. Some other possibilities are:

- Legos
- Small and large cardboard boxes
- Cardboard tubes
- K'nex
- Magnatiles
- Kapla blocks (aka Brain Blox or Keva blocks— one inch by four inch by 1/8 inch planks)
- Zoob building sets
- Straws or sticks with clay balls

Scan the qr code for: one source for unit blocks

In my opinion, it's best to keep any construction materials you offer open-ended, to encourage extended play with the greatest scope for imagination possible. Themed construction sets seem to be popular in toy stores, but following directions to make a pre-determined product is a different mental process from the invention and problem-solving involved in creating from the imagination.

Children can build in two dimensions or three. Infants and toddlers may stack blocks or rocks or small boxes; the material invites it. Preschoolers may create enclosures (flat on the floor) or build the tallest buildings they can with the materials they have. School-aged children continue to find joy in constructing with smaller, more detailed materials, or with wood, hammers, nails, and screws. Construction may be representational ("We're building a castle!"), experimental ("I'm trying to make it balance.") or purely physical (building for the express purpose of knocking down). Through construction, children learn physics, mathematics, spatial reasoning, and literacy concepts (e.g. in the stories they tell as they play with their structures and signs that they make for their buildings). They also develop perseverance, problem-solving ability, motor control, and impulse control through construction play.

Enriching Construction Play

- **Loose parts**

  Any objects that can be combined with any other objects to represent an idea are loose parts. Combining dissimilar loose parts engages the imagination and requires spatial reasoning, problem-solving, and more while being extremely satisfying. For the most part, loose parts are not attached to each other in any permanent way. Rather, the work is primarily arranging the loose parts in pleasing designs or constructions. Your child might decorate her block structure with glass blobs or use rocks to create a walkway into her cardboard box castle, for example. See Appendix for examples of loose parts.

Sometimes children will create their own loose parts to add to a construction, such as signs for a zoo they have made or, as in the image above, stained glass windows for a castle.

Block Stories and Building Tall

Years ago, a colleague and I noticed a difference in the way that the girls at our schools played with blocks and the way the boys played (at age 5). We saw that the boys built as tall as they could and then immediately, without playing with their structures, gleefully knocked their structures down. The girls, on the other hand, spent little time actually building. They created two-dimensional enclosures that sort of mapped out places for the characters to be (little animals or models of people or even just imaginary figures). They created stories, and the construction aspect of the activity seemed to get lost. My colleague and I were intrigued and set out to study how we could get the boys to spend more time reflecting on their process and playing with what they built and how we could help the girls experience the pleasure of, and develop the skills to, engage more deeply in building. What resulted was a change in the kinds of materials and support we offered boys and girls from then on, and enhanced learning for both.

Block stories (what the girls were doing naturally) bring imagination and extended engagement into the construction process. Once a small group of children had begun to build, we would ask what their plan was. When more than one child was building, asking about their plan was often the provocation that either solidified the plan or revealed that there was no agreement on a plan. Conversation took care of that, and once the children agreed on a plan for their structure, they would negotiate other aspects of their building. The stories would come naturally then. ("This is the trap that catches the bad fairy when she comes to take the jewels.") When it felt right, I might comment, "This sounds like a story." If my timing were good, the children would say, "It is a story!" I then offered to write the story down as the children told it. Sometimes they acted their story out as they built, sometimes the story was more like a tour of their structure, and sometimes they would tell a part of the story they hadn't built yet, which inspired them to return to construction.

If your child tells block stories, you can give the stories an importance that matches the learning opportunity that it is. Take a picture of the structure and post it and the story—and maybe even an illustration your child makes to go with it—on the wall or in his journal.

A block story, "Castle in the Sea"

Paper Construction

You need:

- Colored paper
- Heavy paper or cardboard to serve as a base for collage
- Scissors
- Glue or glue stick
- Clear tape
- Pens (optional)

You can invite your child to create two- or three-dimensional constructions with paper. Here are some ideas:

- **Collage**
  For the youngest children:
  If your child is ready for scissors, give her colored paper or a magazine page and let her cut, cut, cut. Invite her to cut paper of varying textures, such as waxed paper, construction paper, or newspaper. She will cut and cut without attending to shapes or pictures, and she will make a big mess, but together you can sweep up the scraps and maybe keep some of them for a later project. In my experience, a child who is just learning to cut or glue rarely does both at the same time.

  Invite your toddler to experiment with "sticking." Introduce glue sticks and let your child glue scraps on a large base of paper/cardboard to his heart's content. You can provide small pieces of paper of different colors and shapes for him to glue onto the board or invite him to use the scraps from earlier cutting experiences. Help him see the base paper as a boundary: the scraps can go anywhere on this surface, but they stop at the edges (i.e. they don't like to get glued onto the table).

For preschoolers and older:

Offer cardboard, cardstock or other heavy board as a base. If your child is already comfortable with scissors and with gluing, she can cut her own shapes out of paper for collage. After she has explored cutting and gluing, she might like to create pictures with collage.

Your child can also cut shapes to glue together to make a figure without gluing it onto a board. Whether she uses a base or not, this work will help your child attend to the parts of things and their relationship to the whole: a head, neck, body, legs, and tail feathers go together to make one turkey. This experience will carry over into understandings such as "letters go together to make one word."

- **Make it stand**

  Ask your child, "Can you make this piece of paper stand up?" Of course, a piece of paper will not stand unaltered. But give your child a chance to try. Then say, "Let's see if we can change it so it will stand up." Your child may think of rolling it into a tube or folding it in some way. Or she may think of something you never would! Explore the possibilities together.

  Later, offer strips of heavy paper of various lengths. Let your child explore how to fold and/or twirl the strips to make the paper stand up.

- **Make a box**

  If your child is showing interest in making houses (or other buildings), support her while she figures out how to make a house (cube) using heavy-weight paper and clear tape. Once she has made a cube, she will discover she can create buildings, cars, or anything that is cube-like in nature.

  In time, your child will begin to use the "alphabet" of paper construction—boxes, paper rolled into tubes, strips, etc.—to make whatever she imagines from paper in two or three dimensions. This alphabet of techniques will allow her to use paper construction as a language for expression.

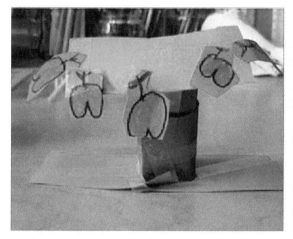

Apple tree

Haunted house

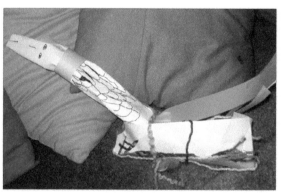

A goose

Small Worlds

When Tristan was little, he spent hours creating small worlds—little scenes made from natural materials and tiny toys. He made homes for the ants he found on our front porch. He made fairy villages under a spreading pine tree. He didn't particularly enjoy blocks or Legos, but he was passionate about small worlds. When he was three, we moved to a new house that had a wonderful window seat at a perfect three-year-old's height. Tristan spent hours creating a world for a two-inch toy giraffe, running from the living room to his bedroom and back again, over and over, to collect materials and create a complex 6-foot-long microworld. Included in the materials he used were some feathers, some paper figures and other lightweight items. And then our rather large greyhound came to investigate and breathed on Tristan's world, blowing it all out of place. Of course, Tristan was incensed, but, accepting our assurances that Abby did not *mean* to destroy his small world, he rebuilt, and we made sure that Abby did not huff and puff near the window seat again.

At school we offered scaffolds for small world play with:

- Platforms for play on multiple levels. Cutting boards of various sizes and shapes work well, as do small tree stumps or larger tree cookies (slices of trunks of small to medium-sized trees)
- Smaller sections of tree trunks or blocks to use as spacers between platforms and tiny tree cookies, which you can cut from branches with garden clippers
- Fabric. We used natural world colors like green and brown, to use as ground or canopy
- Unspun colored wool is a great addition. It often became the top of trees or bushes. (See Appendix for a source for wool)
- Small rocks

- Glass blobs
- Pieces of tree bark
- Small figures: people, animals, dinosaurs, fairies
- Pieces of moss
- Flower fairies (see the section on wire)
- Whatever your child thinks to add

Provide the materials and a space for building (preferably out of reach of any resident greyhounds) and let your child construct.

Sculpting

Representing in three dimensions is qualitatively different from representing in two dimensions. That is, in order to draw a cat you have to understand certain things about "catness." But in order to sculpt a cat in three dimensions, you have to have a different set of understandings. Try it. Draw a cat. Then take some clay and make a cat that stands up. What do you have to think about that you didn't have to think about when you were drawing? By working in both two dimensions and three, your understanding of "cat" deepens. This is one reason we invite children to work in both dimensions. Construction is work in three dimensions, but it is different from clay or wire or other media for sculpture because it involves putting discrete parts together. Clay and wire are often worked in a more continuous way. Found-materials sculpture bridges the two kinds of media: discrete pieces put together in a permanent way.

Clay

You need:

- Clay (see Appendix for a source for clay)
- Table covering. Canvas (from a fabric store or online store) works best. Although clay will stick to them more than to canvas, you can also use paper or paper bags. In the picture above, we have covered a 12"x12" piece of plywood with canvas stretched tight and stapled on the back.

This is all you will need at first. Later:

- Something pointy like toothpicks, skewers, or pencil
- Possibly a rolling pin
- Objects with interesting textures for making impressions, such as shells, buttons, Legos, little pieces of burlap or netting, natural materials, etc.
- Blunt-ended knife

Dough is good for sensory purposes: to squish and poke and flatten. That works for toddlers and young preschoolers, but it is not very satisfying for children who want to represent with the medium. It doesn't stay where you put it very well, and detail gets lost in its squishiness.

I prefer real potter's clay. It is not particularly expensive, often comes in 25-pound bags (so it lasts a long time if you care for it), and it will let your child do much more with it than dough ever will.

I suggest that you introduce clay by itself, with no tools, to your child no matter the age. She will want to explore the clay, possibly many times, before she is ready to represent with it. A toddler's clay repertoire will probably consist of poking, pounding, squishing, rolling, and even using body parts other than hands to manipulate it. This exploration is for learning about the clay. Children a little older will explore the four clay forms (without any prompts from you!): ball, coil (snake), slab (pancake), and pot. When you notice that your child has intent to represent and she is trying to stick pieces of clay together, you can show her how: paint a little water on the ends of both pieces you want to stick together, gently put the pieces together, and then smooth the clay from one piece to the other to look like one piece. When your child needs tools like a plastic knife, toothpicks, etc. in order to accomplish a goal, that's when to offer them.

First experience with clay: poking

And pounding

◄ *After many experiences exploring clay, this five-year-old can use clay as a language to make a cat. She is using as a referent a clay cat made by a small group of children in a previous year's class.*

Ideas for working with clay

- Making Impressions

  Once your child has explored making slabs, you can invite her to make a slab, cut it into a shape (or not), and press small textured objects into it. If you poke a hole in the top and let the piece dry, you have a lovely hanging ornament.

In addition to creating impressions, your child may choose to draw in the clay slab with a wooden skewer, pencil, or other sharp object

- Make it stand

  If your child makes many coils (snakes) all lying down, challenge her to make one that stands up. What can she make with her coil standing up? Similarly, if she is making slab (pancake) after slab lying down, ask if she can figure out how to make a slab stand up. What does it remind her of?

  If she makes many animals in two dimensions, challenge her to make the same thing standing up. This poses a new set of problems for her to solve.

  o What can she make with just coils?

  o What can she make with just slabs?

  o What can she make with coils and slabs together?

- Bas Relief

  Bas relief is a form of sculpture in which figures barely protrude from the background. Show your child some images of bas relief. She can create bas relief figures herself by first making a slab out of clay and then forming figures and attaching them to the slab.

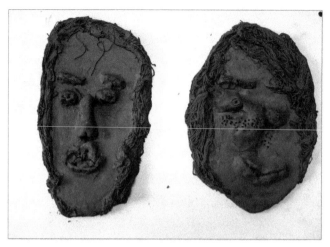

Bas relief portraits in clay sculpted by two 5-year-olds

- Telling a story in clay

    If your child paints or draws a similar story multiple times, you could invite her to also construct the story in clay. She might draw or build a story on a slab. Or she might want to construct a playset with all the characters in a story she knows or a story she writes. Every time she represents an idea in an additional medium or in another dimension, she figures out something new about the process or content. When a child showed us that she was particularly passionate about a topic, story, or idea at school, we liked to encourage her to represent it in as many ways as she was willing to entertain.

◄ *A child made the characters from Charlotte's web out of clay. After they were fired, she painted them. You don't have to fire clay pieces, but they are fairly fragile if you don't. If you don't have access to a kiln, you can use air-dry clay, available at craft stores or online, to make pieces your child wants to keep and play with.*

Let your child's imagination be your guide with clay. It's a particularly flexible medium and, for some children, it is immensely satisfying.

Wire

You need:

- Wire: thin but bendable for small hands. It can be colored (like telephone wire) or metallic. Pipe cleaners are a good first wire, but in time they may not be as satisfying as wire without the fuzz.
- Wire cutters or dedicated scissors that will cut the wire you have.
- A base for sculptures. For some projects, a piece of Styrofoam packing may do. For others, your child may prefer a lump of clay. You can even wind the end of the wire many times around a good-sized rock to stand a sculpture up.
- Wooden beads and pony beads
- "Silk" flowers, taken apart (for flower fairies and tree flowers)

Playing with wire is like playing with lines off the page. It gives children an opportunity to learn another means of attaching, i.e., twisting, and it presents a set of unique challenges.Wire is conducive to stringing, sculpting, attaching, and more. I found that I did have to show children how to twist wire to connect it to itself and let them know that they did not have to tape or glue pieces of wire together. Beyond that, they usually figured out how to create different forms with the wire.

◀ *These sculptures were made with wire, shaped (you can see the children were developing an "alphabet" of wire forms here) and then stuck into foam packing blocks.*

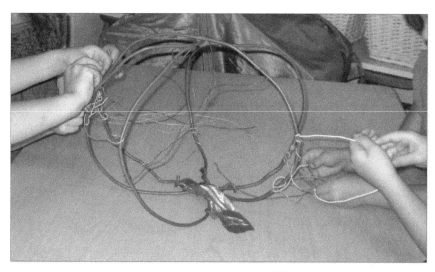

Getting started on the chandelier

For this collaborative project, which the children called "chandelier" and asked for it to be hung over the cubby house, I provided an armature of a sphere made from heavy wire. The children twisted and wove "telephone" wire and beads all around it, changing its shape organically and creating something they declared beautiful.

A five-year-old who had been drawing and painting tree frogs expanded her representation to sculpt one in wire.

Flower fairies and Tree flowers

You need:

- Thin wire like telephone or kraft wire
- Wooden beads for heads
- Silk flowers, taken apart. The flower parts usually have a hole in the middle, making them perfect for stringing.
- Pony beads (I like the colored clear ones)

Materials for making flower fairies. I found a wooden bead car seat cover at a thrift store and cut the hundreds of beads apart, giving us lots of materials for making.

Your child can choose a bead for the head. Then, she can fold the wire in half and feed it through the hole in the head bead, leaving about an inch at the top. She can twist that inch to make a loop for hanging and to keep the head on. Then, holding the two wires together, she can string beads and flowers until the body is long enough. End with a bead. Twist the wire under the last bead to hold the body together. Separate the two wires now and add beads at the ends of the wires for feet if desired. There's really no wrong way to do this, as long as the result pleases your child.

You can hang the flower fairies all over your yard and even surprise some neighbors by hanging flower fairies on their front doors or on neighborhood trees.

Tree flowers

One year the children were searching for a way to console the trees in autumn when they lost their leaves. So, we invited them to make tree flowers in a way similar to flower fairies, but without the heads. These were more abstract than the flower fairies. The children declared that the trees felt much better about losing their leaves after they festooned them with tree flowers.

Aluminum Foil

You need:

- Aluminum foil
- Colored Sharpie markers or acrylic paint
- Balls of clay (for standing sculptures up)
- In addition, for Bas relief work:
- Heavy cardboard base
- Relatively thin (no more than ½ in. thick) recycled objects of varying shapes
- Glue

Aluminum foil is like wire, in that it stays where you put it. It is also like paper, as it comes in sheets. It is reflective, and it accepts Sharpie ink and acrylic paint if your child wants color. With foil your child might:

- Make boats that float
- Make jewelry or hats
- Make sculptures. Make foil figures stand with little balls of clay.
- Make Bas relief sculptures.

Offer cardboard, found objects, and foil. The child glues objects to the cardboard. When the glue dries, she presses foil over the cardboard and objects, creating a bas relief sort of effect. She can color either the protruding parts, the background, or both, with Sharpie or acrylic paint.

Encourage her to explore the possibilities!

Having drawn a plan for a deer they want to make, two children begin to sculpt with foil.

Working on the ears of the deer.

Weaving

You need:

- A loom or frame on which you can create a loom
- Cotton twine
- Long strips of colorful fabric, yarn, colored cellophane, leaves, sticks, etc.

Making things stick

The wonder of weaving is that you can make things "stick" without glue or tape, and even very young children can make it happen. You can make a simple loom with a picture frame. Weaving requires a warp (the strings through which you weave) and the weft (the yarn with which you weave). On an empty picture frame, string the warp, with each string about ¼" from the next.

I made this loom from a discarded card catalogue frame. I installed cup hooks at the top and bottom and then added plastic lacing to make a beginners' loom.

Or, you can buy a lap loom fairly inexpensively (see Appendix for a source)

At first, you will want to provide feathers, sticks, strips of cloth, and anything you think might stay when pushed through the warp, and let your child explore.

Paper weaving

You need:

- Heavy paper (construction paper works well)
- Scissors
- Glue stick

Fold a piece of paper in half like a "hamburger" (the short way). Cut slits about 1" apart through both layers, starting at the fold, to about 1" from the open end. When you open the paper, you should have an intact piece with slits. Cut strips of contrasting paper of one or more colors the length of the short side of the paper (i.e., with 9x12 construction paper, your strips will be 1" wide and 9" long). Your child can weave, "over, under, over, under," being sure to start "over" if the last row ended in under, and "under" if the last row ended in over (i.e., alternating starting positions for each row). She should push the strips she has woven together so that she sees a checkerboard-like pattern. When no more strips will fit, she can glue the ends to the mat, top and bottom, on both sides.

Lap weaving

You need:

- Cardboard looms (See Appendix for a source for looms)
- Cotton twine
- Multiple colors of yarn
- Scissors
- Tapestry needle (blunt, with a big eye)

You can set up a loom with just 5-7 warp strings for the beginner or with more for a wider tapestry. Your child can weave with yarn on a tapestry needle. When he has finished weaving the piece, simply cut the warp strings off the loom and tie two together across the piece.

 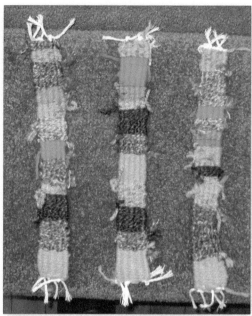

Big and little circle weaving

You need:

- A source for pliable vine or a hula hoop
- Cotton twine
- Raffia or yarn of multiple colors
- Discarded CDs
- Tapestry needle

Once your child is proficient at horizontal weaving, she can weave in the round. If you have a source of willow, wisteria, or other woody vines, you can make a cool circular loom (if not, you can do the same thing with a hula hoop). Create a frame by forming the vine into a circle repeatedly until the frame is as thick as you want it. Weave the ends into the frame. Then, string a warp by tying string to the frame, pulling it to the opposite side of the frame, and wrapping a few times around the frame to secure it. Pull the string back across the center a few inches from the first place the string is tied, and so on all around the frame. We wove onto this frame with different colors of raffia, but you can use strips of fabric or bulky yarn (use your imagination!).

We secured the frame to one of the "windows" of the cubby house (see section on Dress-up and Dramatic Play). Your child can begin weaving from the middle. This is a challenge best undertaken after your child has had many other experiences with weaving.

You can make little circle looms on old CDs or embroidery hoops. String them in the same way that we did for the giant raffia loom, above.

Found looms

- **Fairy looms**

  Find a branch that looks like the letter Y. Wind string horizontally around the "V" section with space between each pass to make the warp. This will be the loom. Your child can weave "over, under, over, under" through the warp either with found materials or with yarn and a tapestry needle.

- **Fencing looms**

  For this you need a fence with space between the slats (a deck fence is perfect). Choose long strips of 2" fabric for this kind of weaving. Your child can weave in and out through the fencing.

- **Laundry basket looms**

  If your laundry basket has holes in the sides, your child can weave in and out of the holes.

- **Baby gate looms**

  Many baby gates make good looms.

Fairy Loom

Weaving without a loom

If you have a source of willow, wisteria or another woody vine, you can explore "dreamweaving" a la Patrick Dougherty.

You need:

- Vine
- Clippers
- Styrofoam base (optional)
- Wire

Scan the qr code for: Patrick Dougherty's work

"A child's world is fresh and new and beautiful, full of wonder and excitement. It is our misfortune that for most of us that clear-eyed vision, that true instinct for what is beautiful, is dimmed and even lost before we reach adulthood."

- Rachel Carson

5 A Relationship with the Natural World: Diving into Wonder

Following Children's Curiosity

Children are born curious. Curiosity is what drives learning, but sometimes schooling teaches a child not to follow his curiosity, and that could hinder the possibilities for engaging in inquiry. When school becomes about figuring out what the teacher wants your child to do and say, *that* becomes the research in which the child engages. If you want your child to attune to his own curiosity and to exercise his right to follow it, you will want to send him the message that you value his curiosity and that to engage in inquiry is worthy of his—and your—time. You can do that by joining him when he exclaims over the ant on the sidewalk and wants to watch it to see where it goes. Engage him in conversation about what he is observing. Try to do this in a way that does not interfere with his intent; when adults take over a child's research the child often lets it go. The idea is to help him realize his own intent and to help him stay engaged.

You may be surprised by changes in your own outlook when you do this. We never really lose the curiosity with which we were born. Rather, it seems to go dormant, to have been driven underground by expectations of academia and adult life. How much we miss! Your child's drive to understand is your ticket to return to your natural state. You get to rediscover long-lost pleasures at his side.

The Natural World

At Richmond's Arts in the Park last Spring, I mentally cataloged the activity of children I thought were between two and three years of age. Here is what I saw: Children in strollers with pacifiers in their mouths, staring blankly ahead despite the activity of the festival. Children, also in strollers, with iPhones (presumably their parents') not even engaging with the world around them.

I also saw some children walking, sometimes holding an adult's hand, but also sometimes stopping to speak to a dog or pick up a pinecone or talk to an artist. They asked questions of their adults. Or engaged in running monologues. These children's adults did have to pay attention; there was nothing tethering the children to them, and the children had their own ideas and agendas. Which children were learning, do you suppose? If you guessed the untethered children, you are right. The engaged child is a learning child; that is true no matter the venue. The natural world offers a deep dive into engagement, and you don't have to do anything but be with your child and follow his lead. He will find what interests him in the woods, or the park, or the back yard. It's an environment that is always changing; something is always happening in nature.

When we moved to a wooded area when Tristan was three, we would walk together on the trails along the James River. I taught him—and we practiced—one thing. When I said, "Stop!" he had to stop on a dime (for safety's sake). Once he had a reliable "Stop!" he could run ahead at his speed (I "stopped" him before he went around any blind corners or got too far). He could explore a puddle or a hole at the base of a tree, or a lovely thick vine hanging from a tree. He observed the way neither the woods nor the river was the same place twice. He developed a relationship with a set of exposed roots on the riverbank, sitting among them, as if in a hug, to arrange pebbles and flowers on the roots. I knew he was learning a lot, but I didn't know how deep an emotional attachment he had to that tree until the river flooded its banks one day when he was four. When the river receded enough to expose the paths again, I took Tristan to see his tree. I foolishly thought he'd be intrigued by the changes he observed. Instead, he burst into tears, in mourning for his tree who, in his eyes, had lost its roots (underwater) and, to his sorrow, would never be the same again. After I made space for his big feelings, Tristan emerged from that experience a bit more philosophical; by talking about his sadness and about what had happened, he constructed some new knowledge about the inevitability of change in the world. I learned, too. I understood in a new way the reciprocity between emotion and intellect that create the best conditions for deep learning. Nowhere is better for this than in nature. An opportunity to develop a relationship with the natural world may be one of the best gifts you can give your child.

Observational Drawing

Your child will learn a great deal by just interacting with the natural world. And she will undoubtedly want to bring pieces of it home with her (I am told that at age 5 I insisted on taking home the tiny dead fish I found floating in a pond in my neighborhood. Apparently, I also insisted that my mother take a picture of me with it, and this is how I remember the incident). When your child finds an object that you think would be good for this purpose, invite her to draw a picture of it. Encourage her to draw what she *sees* (rather than what she already thinks it looks like, especially if it's a familiar object like a flower) and to include everything she sees. It is said that one only sees properly what one has drawn. Observational drawing teaches the eye and the hand, and it expands the mind.

You can also set up a table with something interesting on it, perhaps from nature, and invite your child to draw what she sees. Encourage her to draw not what she knows but what she actually sees, and to look beyond basic forms and include detail. Black Papermate Flair pens (which I call "thinking pens," because when children draw with them they seem to attend more to form, line, and detail than when drawing with other media) facilitate observational drawing best, as the task does involve focus on form and detail. Your child can color her observational drawing later if she wants to.

Observational drawing of a branch and pinecone, in sets of three. My hypothesis is that the child drew three of each in an attempt to master the task she set for herself.

Studying a lizard and a rock through observational drawing

Observational drawing of the outdoor classroom, including the class pet dog, Lucy

Keeping a Nature Journal

You might invite your child to do her observational drawing in a nature journal, a bound book just for her nature observations. She can take it with her on your walks or to the back yard. She can study through drawing the flower arrangement on the dining room table. She can record her lost teeth. She can press flowers or leaves in it. She can paste photographs from your trips into nature in it. Show her how to work from the beginning of the book, one page at a time, and help her write her thoughts about the drawings she puts in the journal (i.e., write her words for her, tell her the letters so she can write, help her when she gets stuck writing the words as they sound, or whatever is appropriate for her stage of literacy acquisition).

Any bound book can serve as this journal. You can even make one yourself by folding several pieces of heavy drawing paper in half and stapling them into book form.

Collecting

Most children love to collect. When we took nature walks in Junior Kindergarten, we often took baskets or bags for this purpose. Every now and again we would agree on the kind of thing we were looking for, but frequently it was free-range collecting. When we got back to the classroom, the children would often sort their finds. I learned to be ready with trays and bowls for this purpose. Once the materials were sorted, we would have a meeting to talk about the children's ideas for the materials. Many a project emerged from collections from nature: Collages, mobiles, fairy houses and fairy villages, or displays in transparent CD cases hung in the windows.

Ice Art

You need:

- Small plastic plate
- Water
- Natural materials: berries, leaves and conifer needles, winter flowers, etc.
- String
- Scissors
- A cold day or space in the freezer

In the Winter, we froze berries and little branches in water on small plates to make tree decorations. The children created little scenes or designs with the natural materials in water on plastic plates. We then made a loop for hanging them by folding a piece of string in half and placing the two ends in the water at the top of the plate. We put the plates outside on a cold day to freeze, and when they were frozen solid, we hung the "ice art" in a tree. The play of the sun on and through the frozen discs was mesmerizing.

Mommy, they're taking away my imagination!

Portrait with natural materials

Fairy house in a fairy garden. The door was a gift from an adult who was impressed by the children's fairy house. We simply placed it in front of the house for the children to discover. For days the children talked about who might have put the door there, with consensus leaning toward the fairies themselves.

Drawing Theories

The children who were considering where the sun goes at night drew their theories after their first conversation to tackle the question. In doing so, they were clarifying for themselves their own theories, and they were working out which of the other theories posed in the conversation they would accommodate into their own theories. You can do this at home, too. Start with your young child by drawing his theory as he is articulating it (a good reason to carry a little notebook and pen with you wherever you go!). Check in with him as you draw: "Is this what you mean?" Show him that drawing is a way of enhancing the understanding of another person when you are posing a theory. As your child develops his drawing ability, you can invite him to draw his theory while or after he explains it, saying, "It helps us both if we can see it."

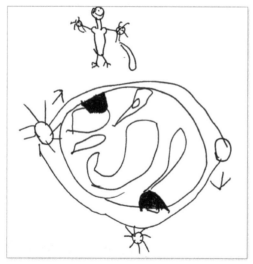

There are 2 suns and 1 moon. The moon moves to the middle sun when it thinks it is morning. The sun trades places with it. The side sun asks the other sun when it's his turn to go to the moon.

The sun goes behind the mountain when the moon is up. God puts it there when it's going to be night.

Try it yourself. Can you draw your theory about how your microwave heats food? Or how your wifi router works? Can you draw your theory about how your child views the world?

Light and Shadow

Window Wonders

You need:

- Clear contact paper
- Scissors
- Colored transparent paper (tissue paper, cellophane, or the like) cut into tiny squares
- Fairly flat natural materials (leaves, flowers, small sticks)
- Other flat materials (see below)

Cut a piece of contact paper to the size desired (no bigger than the window-pane in which you plan to hang it). Tape the contact paper to the table, sticky side up, so that it doesn't move while your child works. Your child can create designs/pictures right on the contact paper with:

- Flowers or leaves or other fairly flat natural materials
- Little squares of translucent colored paper for a mosaic effect or overlapping the edges for a play on color.

You can even cover an entire window with the contact paper so that your child can create an entire window of color with translucent paper, fall leaves, or anything else that will interact with the light from the window. If you choose a sunny window, you may get some beautiful colored shadows all over your room!

Translucent mosaics on tracing paper, created on a light table

Translucent mosaics on clear contact paper

More ideas for window wonders:

- º Different colors of string of various lengths along with buttons, pom-poms, or fairly flat recycled materials

- º Toothpicks or popsicle sticks, which your child can paint first or use as is.

- º Transparent colorful bingo chips (sometimes available at dollar stores).

- º Invite your child to cut shapes out of colored transparent plastic, often sold as file folders and create designs/pictures on either the table or window contact paper canvas. See Appendix for a source for these folders.

- ○ Small dried lentils or beans, in different colors.
- ○ Your child can cut straws to different lengths and create designs on the window easel

What else can your child find that will stick and look beautiful?

Remember, there is power in combining materials and in representing the same idea in different ways!

When your child is finished creating, you can either stick the piece right to the window or attach another clear piece of contact paper to it (sandwiching the artwork).

Shadow Play

Shadows are wonderful things, full of just enough mystery and magic to capture the imagination. They look like you, but they don't have features. They grow and shrink as the day progresses. They are often black or grey, but sometimes, they are colored. You can't pick them up and hold them, yet they are real. Are they alive? Can they decide what to do? Or am I always the boss of my shadow? What is a shadow made of? Where does my shadow go at night and when I go inside? Are there shadows at night? These are all wonders children may have about shadows. Children of any age can explore shadows in challenging ways. All you need is light and a surface.

Overhead projectors are a great light source and have enormous scope for imagination. They are out of favor in the business world, so you might be able to find one in a surplus store or in a school that is warehousing them. Ebay also tends to have used ones for sale. But if you can't find one, you can use any really strong light source for shadow play—a portable LCD projector, or even an old slide projector. Cast its light onto a wall or hang up a plain sheet, and you have what you need for shadow play. Here are some possibilities:

- Offer sheer fabric of various sizes and colors and play music, and your child can make her shadow dance in lovely ways.
- Invite your child to make stick puppets with simple shapes out of cardboard and act out shadow stories.

The children here wrote a play. I acted as scribe as they dictated. Then they created their puppets and acted out the play as I narrated, using their words. This shadow screen was fabric suspended in a frame, so the audience could sit on the other side and saw only the shadows.

Construction shadows

You need:

- Shadow screen, which could be:
    - A sheet over one side of a cubby house, if you've made one
    - A sheet hung on a wall
    - A sheet over a large box or any free-standing large object
    - A blank wall
    - A projection screen at its lowest height (may still be too tall)
    - A sheet hung over a wheeled garment rack

- Light source
    - LCD projector
    - Overhead projector
    - Any very strong light source

- Construction materials (see section on Construction and Appendix)
- Colored transparent materials
    - Magnatiles
    - Sheets of Cellophane
    - Sheets cut from clear colored file folders
    - Blocks with clear centers
    - Bubble wrap
    - Use your imagination!

Your child can build as he normally would, but in front of the shadow screen. When you turn on the light source, his structures take on a new life in shadow. Encourage him to build and refer to the shadows he is making. I suggest that you try this only after your child has had plenty of opportunity to play with shadows and his body, as he will need to explore the medium physically before he is ready to represent with it.

When the sun is streaming into a room, invite your child to build with colored transparent materials on a large white piece of paper.

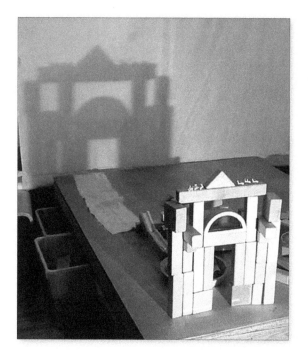 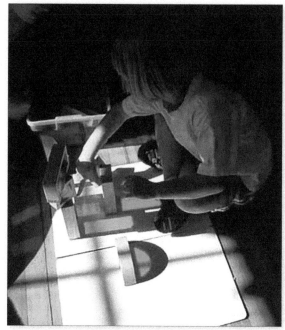

Tracing shadows

You need:

- A sunny day
- Sidewalk chalk
- Three-dimensional objects that will cast a shadow , such as a flower in a pot, large plastic animals, or a structure your child builds with a few blocks or rocks. You might also provide some that cast different shadows, such as a colander or a clear plastic jar.

Your child can set up objects to create interesting shadows and then trace them onto the pavement. If you leave it all there and return to it later, you will have the lovely provocation of both the objects in the same place and the surface in the same place, but shadows someplace else!

A child has lined up model animals with a plan to trace their shadows. She has made a few attempts already but, not satisfied, has relaunched her plan and is trying again.

Children trace each other's shadows on a sunny day

Make a Dark House

"Dark" can feel a little bit dangerous to young children. When offered their own dark space and armed with a flashlight or two, they can experience the power of conquering that danger (and their fear). If you invite your child to represent in some way her experience in the "dark house" (by talking about it, drawing it, etc.), the cognitive process can further regulate the emotion of the experience. This adds to your child's set of personal resources and can make her feel bigger and more in control of her world.

A dark house also gives children a chance to engage in research about light and how it works. Two flashlights are better than one, so that your child can experiment with what happens with light and shadows when one beam joins another. Your child can explore how the distance between light source and surface affects the beam and the shadow, how multiple light sources create multiple shadows, and many other concepts. Use your imagination to provide materials and props in the dark house, adding over time as your child's engagement deepens.

To make a dark house, we covered the cubby house completely with light-blocking fabric. You can create the same effect under a four-legged table by draping it in opaque fabric, cardboard, or black paper. If you have a small room (like a bathroom) with no windows, that would do, too.

Children's research in a "dark house"

Reflection

Mirrors are a gift to the eye and to the mind. Babies learn to recognize themselves in mirrors, toddlers reflect on their own actions through their reflections, and older children explore how reflection works when mirrors are in their environment. Try putting an unbreakable mirror on the floor. Or hinging two mirrors together, putting them on a table, and offering small blocks or plastic lids so your child can build in front of the mirrors. Or hinge three mirrors together to create a kaleidoscope.

Children investigate reflections made by sunlight and a CD.

Three mirrors hinged together as a kaleidoscope create a leap for the eye and for the mind.

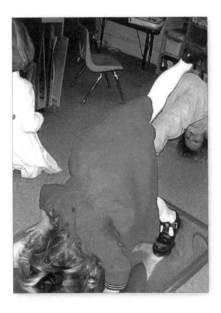

Small, portable mirrors placed in a room with windows on a sunny day invite exploration of reflections cast on walls and ceilings as your child holds them at different angles. Even a sequined shirt or toy can cast wonderful dots of light around a room.

Physics and Engineering

One of the purposes of children's play is to understand the world—how people in their society interact, how to master scary or confusing emotions, and how the laws of physics work, for example. Long-favored children's activities like swinging, walking on low walls, and building with blocks are heavily weighted toward exploring concepts such as perpetual motion, friction, balance, mathematical relationships, and gravity.

Ramps and balls

Ramps and balls offer children rich ground for research about force, gravity, speed, and friction. The youngest children can explore one ramp and a soft ball. Older children can work with multiple ramps, many kinds of balls, and loose parts to add complexity to the experience. Eventually, your child may advance to making sophisticated Rube Goldberg machines. The possibilities for play and learning are endless. Equipping such play is quite simple.

You need:

- Little balls (a variety of materials and sizes is best: rubber, wooden, golf balls, marbles, and wool are good choices).

- Various lengths of plastic gutter and/or cove molding, available at any home improvement store

- Long, sturdy cardboard packing tubes and/or pvc pipe of various lengths with diameters large enough for at least some of your balls

- If you are lucky enough to have or find some clear tubing wide enough to accommodate your balls, all the better.

- Some boxes, blocks, or chairs to support the ramps. You can also cut holes at various heights in a larger box to make a "swiss cheese box." Your child can prop one end of a gutter in any of the holes in the box to make his ramp.

Choose materials with consideration for the age of your child. Tiny balls can be a choking hazard for children likely to put them in their mouths. Balls made of natural wool are perfect for toddlers. For older children, the greater the variety, the greater the possibilities for research. You can provide cars as well, but in my experience, the play can become more about dramatic play with cars than experimentation with what the ramps enable.

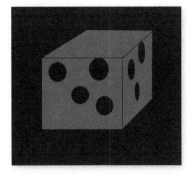

Swiss Cheese Block

Simply provide the materials and your child will take it from there. You might want to demonstrate for a toddler that she can combine the ramp and the ball, but older children will figure out what to do on their own. Eventually, they will begin to expand the possibilities and challenge themselves by using a couch, table, or chairs to vary the incline of a ramp, or find objects to use as stops or barriers.

A hill provides an incline for ramps-and-balls research.

This is a metal wall, with various magnetized ramps, stoppers, and rings.

These children are creating systems with ramps, balls, and blocks.

Materials for play with ramps and balls, all home-made or found (e.g., the rack is actually a wine rack) in use in a Title One public school where funds for such materials are not available.

Chain Reactions

Once children's imaginations are captured by ramps and balls (i.e., the movement of objects without the child exerting force), chain reactions are a natural progression. Your child might start by standing identical blocks on end like dominoes and pushing just the first one, enjoying the chain reaction as they fall in sequence. In time, he might want to add different levels, balls, and special effects to make Rube Goldberg creations.

Scan the qr codes for: Left: Rube Goldberg easy examples & Right: Audri's Rube Goldberg Monster Trap

You might want to check out Kodo Kids (www.kodokids.com) ; their products are expensive, but beautiful. The site will give you ideas about possibilities with ramps and balls as well as other open-ended materials for play (e.g., they have a rubber ramp that can add an uphill component to a ramp run, inviting the child to think about force and incline in a deeper way).

Children discover the power of momentum. They experiment with the placement of a rubber ramp, trying to make the ball go uphill after it gathers momentum while going down.

Invention and Engineering

When we talk about engineering with children, we are referring to the process by which they design and create structures, machines, or inventions. These things occur in play, of course, and we do not need to impose any particular structure on that play. But sometimes we get opportunities to help children experience the language and process of design in a more scientific way.

Tinkering

Creating from found/recycled materials is a wonderful thinking experience. One aspect of tinkering for young children is creating something permanent (i.e. glued or taped together) with found materials. Because this usually involves some skill with tape, the youngest children will probably spend some time exploring the possibilities of "sticking." Give your toddler a surface (such as a big box) and strips of tape to move from one place to another. In doing this, he is constructing a theory of how tape works so that later he can use it to construct. Once your child understands tape and how it works, he can begin to use it to stick things together. For example, he will need to understand that if he puts two objects next to each other, the tape has to attach to both pieces if they are to stay together. He will learn this when he applies tape to only one piece and his expectations that the pieces will be attached are dashed. Try to help him only if he starts to get frustrated (don't wait too long, but also don't assume he won't figure it out). Your role in that process is to provide materials and tools as needed and help only if frustration is looming.

Sticking two-dimensional things together is much easier than sticking three-dimensional things together. Taping three-dimensional objects together requires a skill set of its own. When children first begin to put three-dimensional objects together, such as tissue boxes, tubes, and other recycled materials, they will do what they do when they first work with any medium: they will explore the possibilities. What will these materials do and what will they let me do? The physical act of attaching and the seductive draw of the materials are likely to consume the child's attention at first.

Eventually, however, your child will begin to declare intent to make something. It is at that point that you can invite her to draw a plan for what she wants to make. As you discuss the drawn plan, she can think about the materials she wants to use. As she builds, she can refer to her plan: is it going as she'd thought? Does she need to make changes to her plan?

I am reminded of a project two small groups of Kindergartners did in a public school in which I was consulting. Early in the year, the children were inspired by a box in the classroom, and they asked if they could use it to make a robot. The children had few prior experiences with any of the materials they chose, including tape. Still, they persevered and built a robot with which they were satisfied. The robot went on display in the classroom, but after several months, it was getting worse for wear. "Should I throw it out?" the teacher asked me. I suggested she ask the children. When she did, she was surprised that the children insisted on trying again to build a robot. By then, the children were more competent with tape and with working in three dimensions. Their plan was more complex (two robots, a girl robot and a boy robot) and detailed, and the resulting robots were much more satisfying for the children. This is an example of the reiteration of the engineering process. "Fail forward," they say, for success is born of failure.

Robot number 1, created by 5-year-olds, most of whom had never tinkered before.

Dog treat machine, created by a five-year-old with some experience with tinkering

Two children collaborate to construct a tv with cardboard tubes.

The engineering process (for children with intent to make something specific):

Have an idea

Construct a plan (usually through drawing)

Create a prototype (for young children this is often the one and only version)

Review: Does it do what I want it to do? For young children, this often is more about explaining the creation and how it works and sometimes discovering something "missing" or not attached well. Sometimes this step involves getting feedback from peers.

Relaunch: revise or, sometimes, start again.

The process is cyclical, repeated until the children are satisfied.

Working with four- and five-year-olds, we most often asked them to draw a plan for their invention, articulate in some way what materials they needed, and then begin to construct. Sometimes, the reason for an invention is that the child has identified a problem. For example, when Tristan was in Kindergarten, he invented and drew a machine that would serve as an extra arm and hand for his teacher (including a watch on her arm), because he perceived that she was too busy and could use the help.

Children never love it when they must stop playing and clean up. One group of Junior Kindergartners decided to do something about the problem. They invented a toy-picking-up-machine to do the work for them. For these five-year-olds, we adjusted the engineering process. They drew plans, negotiated about whether the machine would look human or not, figured out what materials they would use, constructed the robot (including inner "workings" made of gears, wire, and a coin slot), solved problems along the way, and presented the finished product to others. The process was not as formal as it might have been for older children, but it had all the components of both engineering and invention.

Two children's images of what a toy-picking-up machine should look like. This was one of many subjects for negotiation involved in the process of making the machine.

The creators of the toy-picking-up machine demonstrate how it works. You pay money, the gears start to work to make the feathers at the top create wind, and the wind sucks up the toys through the arm-like tubes.

If you are at home with one child, she would not have the opportunity to negotiate with others on an invention like this. But elements of invention and engineering are possible.

- Perceiving a problem and having the initiative to do something about it

- Designing a solution. If your child uses drawing as a language, she can draw a plan and talk it through with you.

- Negotiating materials. In the toy-picking-up-machine story, the children thought that metal might be the best material with which to build. We had to negotiate around that because we did not have enough metal at school. The children's solution was based on reality: boxes painted to look like metal and metal "arms." This is negotiation in which you can engage with your child based on what you have, what's practical and safe, and what you are willing/able to procure.

- Construction of the invention

- Trying it out. Of course, many inventions of young children work only with the addition of their magical thinking. Your primary job here is to help your child realize her intent. Don't make it for her, but help her where (and only where) she needs help. Don't place your standards on her product, but support her until she is satisfied.

- Relaunching if your child is not satisfied with the results. That could look like true dissatisfaction. It could also seem as if your child is happy with her invention but then turns around and wants to do it again.

Responding to Your Child's Expressions of Curiosity

How you respond verbally to your child's expression of curiosity will determine whether he remains engaged in his research and in conversation or if he loses interest and answers you with one word.

Instead of:
"Why did your building fall down?"
Try:
"What happened?"

Instead of:
"Eww, a toad!"
Try:
"We almost didn't see that toad! Do you want to stay and watch it?"

Instead of:
"Daddy's busy now."
Try:
"Would you like to draw what you see, and we'll talk about it later, when I'm finished with my phone call?"

Instead of:
Stepping on the spider
Try:
Helping your child catch it and let it go outside, where it would "rather be." Then let your child watch the spider for a bit to see what it does.

"Imagination is more important than knowledge. Knowledge is limited. Imagination encircles the world."

- Albert Einstein

6 More Invitations for the Imagination

Imagination and Intellect

Imagination and intellect are inextricably linked. Along with imagination, though, growth of the intellect requires flexible thinking and emotional flexibility. Flexibility of thinking and emotional flexibility are byproducts (and goals) of the kind of imaginary play and representation suggested in this book. Such flexibility enables an individual (child or adult) to engage in creative problem solving, to be persistent, to follow through on plans, to think of a plan B when plan A fails, to invent, and in general to be a thinking individual. Is this not what we want for our children? Here are a few games you can play with your child that foster cognitive and emotional flexibility.

Songs

Change the words of familiar songs or sing songs that require a creative response.

For example, to the tune of "Here we go 'round the mulberry bush," sing:
    What would you do if I gave you a rope,
    Gave you a rope
    Gave you a rope?
    What would you do if I gave you a rope?
    The child sings the last line,
    I would _____

Then she gets to sing to you, and you have to come up with another way to use a rope. And so on. This song is best when sung over and over; each time you have to come up with new ways to use the rope. You can wonder what you would do with a rope, a hole, a rock, some string, a box, some paper, a tooth—the more creative the better.

An example of changing words to a song:

Assuming your child knows "Mary Had a Little Lamb," sing "Mary had a little _____" and invite your child to decide what Mary should have. For example, if he says, "duck," the rest of the song has to be about the duck. "Mary had a little duck, little duck, little duck, Mary had a little duck, its beak was orange as _____." And so on.

Play the Squiggle Game

You draw a squiggle, and your child draws in order to turn the squiggle into something. Then she draws the squiggle and you turn it into something. You can also do this with large letters or numbers.

Changes

Play "What do you know that changes?"
Your child names all the things that he knows change and tells how they change. For example, a caterpillar turns into a butterfly; a shadow changes its size because the sun moves; a leaf changes color in fall; a mouth changes because you lose teeth.

Imagine "opposite day." How would things be different? In the morning, you would go to bed. You'd eat dinner for breakfast. And so on.

Perspective

In the car, in the bath, any time you have each other's undivided attention, these talking games are fun and encourage flexibility of thinking.

"What would be a giant to a giraffe?" What would be a giant to an ant?" etc.

"What could be a house for a mouse?" "What could be a house for a fairy?" (note this is not what is a house for a mouse, but what *could* be)

"If hungry/silly/frustrated were a color, what color would it be?"

Any of the above can also be turned around. For example, in the house game, if I say "walnut shell" your child can think of what could make a walnut shell a home. Or in the giant game, if I say "mouse," your child can think of what would consider the mouse a giant.

You can also play around with theory of thought. For example, you could ask, "What do you think that butterfly/the wind/the worm is thinking?"

Tristan and I would often play the "I love you more" game. We'd take turns saying, "I love you more than the eagle loves the sky" or "I love you more than the wave loves the ocean," thinking of a new "I love you" for each turn.

Transformations

Attending to transformations requires flexibility of thinking. Cooking is all about transformation: flour, water, and butter become a pie crust, for example. When you involve your child in cooking and baking, she gets to experience transformations, especially if you engage her in conversation about the changes she has witnessed. Here are some other ways to play with transformation.

Transforming the self

Glue a whole-body photo of your child onto cardstock. Invite him to transform his image into a character he likes. Make it stand up by bending a large paper clip to 90 degrees and taping the short loop onto the back of the cardstock at the bottom. Or attach the transformed photo to a block for play.

This child transformed her image into characters from "Frozen."

Another way to encourage your child to see herself in a new way is to invite her to create a mask that is part her and part not-her. For this, you will need a close-up photograph of your child's face looking directly at the camera. Print the photograph (we always did this in black and white) as life-sized as you can make it. Clip a piece of acetate (stiff, clear plastic) to the photograph. Invite your child to trace first the shape of her face, and then the features—eyes, nose, mouth—with a black Sharpie pen. This may be a good challenge, in that your child may want to draw the kind of face she usually draws, rather than trace what she actually sees. Let her check to be sure she has drawn all the parts she needs by lifting the acetate and reviewing her drawing without the photograph behind it. When she is satisfied that she has drawn everything, she can add color and disguise her image in any way she likes. This will become a mask that, because of the transparent nature of the acetate, will look a little like her and a little not like her.

 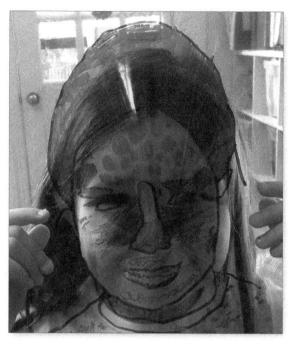

Transforming colors

Provide a clear plastic cup half full of water on a waterproof surface. Give your child an eye dropper and small jars of liquid watercolor. She can experiment with how the water transforms when she adds a color and how it transforms again when she adds a different color. Encourage her to name the colors she creates. Eventually, the water will be "yucky," at which point she can dump it and start again. Older children can record their findings through drawing (i.e., red and blue made purple). Or you can extend this experience by offering coffee filters. Once your child has a color she likes or has never seen before, she can drop some of the color onto the filter and watch it spread. When it dries, she will have a tangible record of her experiments.

Younger children may have trouble with the eyedropper, in which case you may have to fill the dropper so they can squeeze the liquid out.

What other ideas can you or your child think of for liquid watercolor, water, eyedropper, and filters?

Kirigami

Kirigami is the Japanese art of folding and cutting paper. I have found that it helps children become untethered from expectations, because you can't predict what you will get when you open the paper at the end.

It was helpful when a child had too high a satisfaction bar and was never pleased with her efforts. With kirigami, you just can't know what you'll get.

You need:

- Origami paper or regular letter-weight paper of any color.

    Try cutting the paper into a square at first. Later your child can experiment with circles or rectangles.

Show your child how to fold the paper, corner to opposite corner, hold it still, and crease. Fold it again diagonally and crease, and so on. She can fold the paper as many times as she wants. The more times she folds it, the fancier her kirigami will be. However, if she folds it too many times, she will have difficulty cutting through the layers.

Every time she folds, she should fold corner to corner and crease the fold well.

Then she cuts small shapes through all the layers, taking care to leave some space between the shapes.

Children often begin by making single cuts and find the results uninspiring. Show your child how she can cut a little shape every time so that the result when the paper is unfolded is a shape and not just a slit.

Collaborative Storytelling

What you need:

- Nothing to play the game, but a voice recording app on your phone might be welcome.

This is a great game to play in the car, when you are waiting somewhere, or at bedtime. It goes like this:

> *Dad: Once upon a time there was a...*
> *Child: Dragon!*
> *Dad: Who was very...*
> *Child: Sad!*
> *Dad: Because...*
> *Child: He wanted a friend, but his best friend moved to Chicago.*
> *Dad: So one day he...*
> *Child: Went looking for a friend. But he couldn't find one and couldn't find one.*

> *Dad: But then…*
> *Child: A little boy was walking down the street. The dragon said, "Will you be my friend?" The boy said, "Yes, if you don't fire on me."*
> *Dad: So they're walking together down the street and…*
> *Child: A monster came!*
> *Dad: The monster…*

And so on. When there are two or more children playing with a parent, even greater mental and emotional flexibility is required, because the story may not go the way one child had expected. This game can result in stories that can be adapted to plays or puppet shows or a collection of your child's stories, perhaps even illustrated.

"So it is in many situations, especially when one sets up challenges, children show us they know how to walk along the path to understanding. Once children are helped to perceive themselves as authors or inventors, once they are helped to discover the pleasure of inquiry, their motivation and interest explode."

- Loris Malaguzzi (p. 44)

7 Frequently Asked Questions

What About Reading and Writing?

Where is literacy learning in all of this? The child with an awake mind, fostered by all that is in this book, will likely find academic endeavors natural and learn without struggle, as long as invitations are in his environment. That is, if you read to your child daily, answer his questions about print, let him see you reading and writing, and make available books and materials for writing as well as resources such as an alphabet for him to use as reference, he will want to learn to read and write. That desire is made from both the rich environment and his developmental state. The more pleasure and power the child experiences from literacy experiences, the more he will want to engage with print. So, no need for flashcards or workbooks. They can be counterproductive. Think more about:

- Lap reading all kinds of books…storybooks, nonfiction, rhyming books, poetry, etc. Provide a variety of genres, levels of sophistication, and let your child choose what book to read often. Read together every day if you can.

- Developing language through real conversation

- Telling collaborative stories

- Letting your child see literate activities in real life

- Drawing and dictating stories. After your child draws a picture, ask if he'd like you to write his story for him. When you write your child's story as he tells it, you can "think out loud" every now and again, saying, "Beach…b, b, b…Beach starts with B" as you write it. Once he is comfortable with creating these stories, he can start moving toward writing. Ask him, "What's the most important word in your story?" and help him write it. If he doesn't know how to write any of the letters, you can write the word on a card and he can copy it (or you can write it in yellow marker and he can trace it). If he knows some letters, you can dictate the letters and provide him with an alphabet strip to use as a referent. Once he knows some consonant sounds, he can write the words the way they sound. As your child becomes comfortable writing one word for each story on his own, he can start writing two words, then three. Eventually, he is likely to cast you aside and write his stories by himself. Continue to preface his writing with hearing and writing his story for him until he is writing his own stories; you don't want to lose the storytelling aspect of writing in the process of your child's acquisition of the mechanics of writing.

- Painting and dictating stories

- Making signs for block structures, labels for storage bins, or whatever in the house could use a sign for real or play purposes. Your child can do as much of the writing as she can for herself; you can be her "sous writer."

- Writing captions in your child's journal. Again, you can write for your child before she can do it herself, but draw her into the process, showing her what writers do, asking her what a word begins with if you think she knows, and so on. When she knows letters, you can dictate to her the letters of the words she wants to write.

- Taking people's orders in the dramatic play restaurant. This she writes herself!

- Making books (see section on opportunities for drawing)

- Answering her questions about letters, sounds, words, and what readers do

- Ask a children's librarian to direct you to books at your child's reading level, beginning with pre-emergent (maybe one word on a page that corresponds to the picture), emergent (predictable, probably repetitive text with natural language and pictures that correspond to the text), and so on. The librarian should be able to guide you if you tell her what your child is doing. I suggest limiting phonetically regular texts; in order to make all the words in the book fit a phonetic pattern, they don't have natural language and the child cannot use what she knows about language to figure out the text.

Readers learn to read by reading and writers learn to write by writing. The trick is to know how to help a non-reader begin to read (choosing those predictable, repetitive, and/or rhyming books at first, for example) and a non-writer begin to write (see dictating stories, above).

> *If your child is in school, the expectation will likely be that she begin to read in Kindergarten or first grade. However, the range for beginning reading is between ages 4 and 8 and is highly individual. The child learning at home can learn to read according to his own timetable. But the child in school who is not reading according to the school's schedule is likely to experience feelings of inadequacy, lose confidence, and may struggle to participate in what other children are doing. This can create reading difficulties where, actually, there were only differences in the child's timetable due to development and/or interest. Regardless of your child's learning situation, the suggestions here can help her attain literacy in a natural, purposeful, joyful way.*

What About Math?

Mathematics is the study of spatial and numerical relationships. So much of children's play requires them to invent those relationships. Yes, children need to know the names of numbers and what they look like, but that is a tiny fraction of mathematical knowledge. Everything else has to be constructed mentally by the learner. We know that the best way for children to construct this knowledge is through play. When your child is sorting her collection of rocks or shells or leaves, she is creating sets. When she figures out she needs one more plate if every one of her dolls has a place at the table, she is comparing. When she makes a snake of blocks with intent to make it span the room, she is measuring. Your job, as a parent facilitator, is to 1. Notice 2. Offer mathematical language ("Oh! You're SORTING the leaves!" or "Do you need one MORE?") and 3. Be ready to provide more or alternative materials if needed. If your child has developed a deep enough understanding that two plus two equals four, it will be easy for her to represent the idea symbolically (2+2=4) later. That depth of understanding comes from many experiences with mathematical relationships through play and real-world experiences.

You can also:

- Play counting games that require your child to construct one-to-one correspondence between a number and an object. For example, count the giant steps you take together on your way to the car. Next time, count how many baby steps.

- Stay attuned to opportunities to help your child associate quantity with number. In order to count objects, she has to construct the understanding that you can name how many of an object you have by saying the number you stopped on when you were counting, e.g. "One, two, three, four shells. You have FOUR shells." If you pay attention, you will notice myriad opportunities for counting throughout everyday life.

- Play "Who has more?" You can play this game in myriad ways. One way is that each player grabs a handful of something (chips, Legos, rocks, candy) from a bag or box. Each player first estimates whether she has more or fewer objects than the other player(s). Children with more experience with numbers might also like to estimate how many they have without counting. Then everyone counts the objects in turn (the player points or moves each object and says the numbers; the others say the numbers with him). You can take this game as far as you like, perhaps even graphing or recording in another way the numbers for each round, or adding everyone's objects together and counting.

- Make up your own math games. Better still, encourage your child to invent some!

What if My Child Does Worksheets All Day at School?

This is a reality for many children, despite the fact that research does not support the practice—thus, the title of this book! No child should feel he is losing his imagination because of school. If that is the case for your child, you will want to be sure that he has plenty of time to engage with rich materials (and his imagination) at home. Tristan's story is the best example I have. I remember that he constructed a machine to trap shadows out of construction paper at home one evening during his Kindergarten year. I guess he thought those shadows were too elusive! He and his granny once turned her whole living room into a giant spider web, and she let it stay so he could continue to work on it much longer than I would have! He also came to me one day with a CD on which he had placed a little plastic baby and said "Look, Mommy, I'm surfing the web!" Long after he had outgrown the window seat small worlds, he created little villages under a spreading pine tree. After he read, "Bridge to Terabithia" in third grade, he and a friend created a big world for themselves in a ravine next to our house, which they called "Carabithia." It had a hospital, homes, and more that I am not remembering. To this day, he calls that piece of land "Carabithia." Also in third grade, he heard two children arguing in a stairwell. He said to me later that it sounded like opera. The next thing I knew, he had written an aria inspired by the experience and asked me to notate it for him. He started and edited a third-grade newspaper, writing articles he thought were newsworthy and soliciting articles and artwork from classmates. His creativity and ability to come up with good ideas spread to his friends, and this is where a highly introverted child found his leadership ability. All of this happened outside of his school's agenda. Once they have experienced connecting to their imaginations and feeding their intellects, children are driven to continue, no matter where they are.

Tristan's school did not support his style of creativity. Yes, he got to play the violin and go to art class at school. But those were experiences directed by adults. A good analogy is the difference between free play at recess and organized sports. Both may have children moving their bodies outdoors, but only one comes from the child, and therefore, only that one leads to an agile, awake, inventive mind.

How Will This Kind of Education Prepare My Child for Today's World?

First, your child is a citizen of the world right now. We are not preparing her to live in today's world, because she is living in today's world. It is true, however, that we must prepare ourselves to participate in the education of our children for the world they will live in. These days, information is available to anyone who has a cellphone or a computer. Education should no longer be about accumulating a body of facts. What children need to know now is where to find information and, once found, what to do with it. They need to think critically and creatively, be flexible cognitively and emotionally, have the confidence, initiative, and skills to communicate well, the persistence to "see it through," and the social skills necessary to collaborate and lead a team. Too many schools still focus on 19th-century curricular paradigms; high stakes testing has done its part to perpetuate this. If schools must produce children who can pass tests that require more regurgitation than thinking in order to keep their funding, a focus on critical thinking, creativity, and initiative is not going to be high on the agenda.

School is the perfect place for the kind of education I'm proposing, because there are groups of children at school (how else can you collaborate or develop social or leadership skills but with other people?). There are some schools where this kind of education is happening. If you have found one, the ideas in this book can help you create a continuum of learning between home and school. If your child is not in such a school, you can seize the opportunities you have at home to make a positive change in her intellectual life.

What if I'm Homeschooling?

If you are homeschooling permanently, you will want to find other ways for your child to develop the dispositions and habits of mind that are more social in nature. Perhaps you can find other homeschool families who would like to re-imagine their children's education in similar ways and find ways for the children to work collaboratively. Even if it's not on a daily basis, I propose that, given an opportunity to be with peers, a child who has lots of good ideas has a better chance of figuring out how one makes suggestions that don't put people off or how one leads a project successfully than a child who is used to being told what to do at every turn.

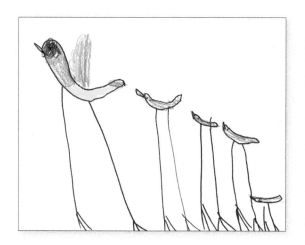
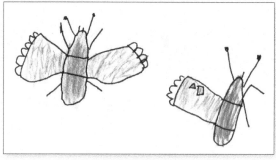

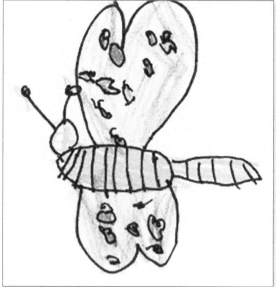

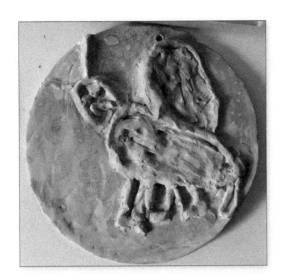

"...if I were asked to name the most needed of all reforms in the spirit of education, I should say: 'Cease conceiving of education as mere preparation for later life, and make it the full meaning of the present life."

\- John Dewey

8 Final Thoughts

The Power of Passion

Consider for a minute your image of schooling. It probably consists of "subjects," right? English, Math, History, and so on. Have you considered that this might not be the best way to organize an education? That there are commonalities among the subjects, and ways of knowing that transcend categories? Could it be a better use of time to learn how to learn than to memorize content that slips away after the test? To learn how to think, to solve problems, to persist, to plan and follow-through, to collaborate and think with others, to imagine and invent, to develop a personal satisfaction bar, to communicate and articulate one's thinking with confidence? These are things that can be learned as a child pursues on a deep level what interests him, something usually unavailable to him at school. I remember the time Tristan, then in third grade, expressed frustration that "just as something is getting interesting in school we have to move on to the next thing." Children learning at home do not have to leave what's interesting.

I've heard it said that very young children have short attention spans. In my experience that is not true. They may have limited interest in what we adults are interested in, but I've observed many three-year-olds spend long periods of time on something that captures their imaginations and feeds their intellects, and the five-year-olds I taught would often return to a project of their design every day for weeks. They learned more than I could have taught them through any traditional curriculum; the breadth and depth of their study of what most interested them were greater than adults have learned to expect from children. In addition, unlike in the traditional school curriculum, the children's projects transcended subject matter. One long investigation of the source of snow with the children in my class, for example, required forming hypotheses, arguing theories (and learning to have cognitive conflict without emotional conflict), experimenting (to make snow), failing, doing research (asking older students how snow is made), engaging with geometry, writing, persisting, exploring shadows (to make a shadow play of the growth of a snowflake), problem-solving, attending to detail (tracing photographs of actual snowflakes), and more. The children's interest and research lasted many weeks—all winter, really, after the first major snowfall in several years in our area, because they were passionate about the research.

At one point, the children decided to ask the 5th graders how it snows. They were certain the big kids would know, because they were the oldest children in the Lower School. The 5th graders were sure they would know, too, because, as one told us, "We had that in 3rd grade." What they had in third grade was exposure to information; they either read the facts or were told them. What they did not have in third grade, it seemed, were the experiences that would have helped them develop a deep understanding of how it snows, and they hadn't studied snow because they were interested, but because it was in the curriculum. As it turns out, the 5th graders' theories about the source of snow were no more sophisticated than those of the 5-year-olds, and the Junior Kindergarten children knew it! After meeting with the fifth graders and hearing their theories about how it snows, they dismissed the older children's theories as implausible and went back to the drawing board. In the end, the five-year-olds came up with a theory that we adults would recognize as close to accurate, one that they could build on as they grew, and one they would not forget. Many years later I spoke with one of the children in that group, then a senior in high school. She had chosen her college for its stellar physical science opportunities. When I reminded her of her role in the Snow investigation in Junior Kindergarten, she said, "That's where my passion for science began!"

Images from the shadow play, "How It Snows," in which five-year-olds constructed the growth of a snowflake

Conclusion

Whether you are educating at home temporarily, homeschooling on a permanent basis, or just want to support your child to learn in ways not available in school, you can help your child feed her intellect and develop the dispositions and habits of mind that will help her keep forever the enthusiasm for learning with which she was born. And you can both have a marvelous time doing it.

Your own stance will shift from telling to listening. From leading to walking alongside your child. From "teaching" to facilitating, challenging, and providing materials. You will become a fellow traveler on the learning journey and, in doing so, come to see your child in a whole new light.

I hope you will use whatever you find useful in this book as inspiration and as a springboard. There is no way I could ever have included *all* the possibilities. Use your imagination. Follow your child's imagination. Be kind to yourself. Remember: the most experienced teachers offer provocations that fail every now and again. Let me hear how it's going. Perhaps we can start a conversation that goes beyond schooling. And above all, never let your child fear that he might lose *his* imagination.

Appendix

MATERIALS TO HAVE ON HAND

Paper

Any parent of a young child has experienced the allure of paper. But have you thought about the kinds of paper you offer? Papers with different weights, textures, shapes, and sizes suggest different possibilities.

For example:

- Unlined paper
- Cardstock
- Colored tissue paper
- Construction paper
- Waxed paper
- Watercolor paper
- Grid paper
- Tracing paper
- Cardboard, smooth and corrugated
- Clear contact paper

◄ *A child plays with an extra-long piece of packing paper, saved from a shipment box.*

Paper is not the only canvas good for drawing or painting. Think about:

- Discarded CDs
- Foil
- Transparent plastic (acetate), such as is used for transparency projection, available at office supply stores or amazon.com
- Rocks
- Labels
- Recycled materials

Drawing media

- Washable markers, fat and thin
- Construction paper crayons (They show up on light or dark paper!). For toddlers just developing an effective grip, fat crayons are sturdier.
- Black Papermate Flair pens (which I call "thinking pens," because when children draw with thinking pens they seem to attend more to form, line, and detail than when drawing with other media). Thinking pens are not washable.
- Colored pencils
- Sharpies (They make satisfying marks, but, like thinking pens, have permanent ink). Sharpies are needed if drawing on foil, plastic, or other smooth or shiny material.
- Oil pastels
- Chalk (sidewalk chalk and regular colored chalk)

Paint

There are so many kinds of paint! Here are a few.

- Watercolor, either in cake form or liquid. You can get Sax Liquid Washable Watercolors on Amazon.com

- Tempera (Sometimes this is called poster paint)
- Acrylic paint (best if you are painting rocks or something that needs to be water-resistant)
- Finger paint
- Water. Just painting a wooden fence or slates on a walkway with water can be quite satisfying…and you get to watch your painting disappear as the water evaporates.

Paintbrushes

- I like Royal Brush Big Kids brushes for young children because the handles are short and plastic (vs. painted wood; the paint always seems to peel off after a few scrubbings) and they come in many widths. The youngest children may find the wider brushes more satisfying. But older children will need to be able to choose a brush for the kind of line they intend to paint: wide for large areas, small for detail.

Office supplies

- Tape of all kinds. Lots of tape. For example:
  - Masking tape (comes in plain manila and colors)
  - Clear "scotch" tape
  - Duct tape
  - Washi tape
- Liquid glue
- Glue sticks
- Stapler and staples
- Hole punches
- Scissors that will cut paper and fabric. Fiskars child-sized scissors with blunt ends work well.
- Clipboards, for taking drawing/writing outdoors or to other places without a table

- Fasteners (paper clips for standing figures up; brads for attaching pieces that move)

Clay

- I like white low-fire potter's clay without grog. You can get it online, but I'd only order it if I couldn't get it in town or if I could get free delivery.

  See the section on clay for tools you might want to have on hand.

Fabric

I get my fabric mostly from sewing leftovers and thrift stores. You might want:

- Large, drapey (sheer curtains are great for this) fabric and clothespins or tablecloth clips
- Small and larger pieces of solid fabric and pieces with intriguing patterns
- Fabric with a variety of textures
- Here is a good source of fabric sized for making swings and hammocks that can weather the elements outdoors.

For big wooden clips to use with the fabric. You can get Camden Rose Cherry Play Clips on Amazon.com.

Scan the qr code for: Source for large format, strong fabric

Wire

- Lightweight colored wire like Twisteez wire or "telephone" wire can be found on Amazon.com.
- You can get Silver Aluminum Flexible Armature wire on Amazon.com.

PART 8: Final Thoughts

- Darice Craf Wire can also be purchased on Amazon.com.
- Pipe cleaners (available in multiple lengths and in many colors).

Accessories for working with wire, available in craft stores and online

- "Silk" flowers that can be taken apart. Available in dollar stores and craft stores.
- Beads
- Big wooden beads for fairy heads.
- Pony beads for flower fairies.
- Wire cutters for thicker wire
- Dedicated scissors for twisteez wire

Weaving

- Cardboard looms. You can get inexpensive INOVART Cardboard loom at Amazon.com.
- Wooden looms. You can get an inexpensive Melissa and Doug inexpensive loom at Amazon.com.
- Strips of fabric with different textures
- Strips of cellophane
- Natural materials
- A variety of colors, textures, and widths of yarn
- Cotton twine

Construction supplies

Constructive Playthings (CP-U312) unit blocks can be purchased on Amazon.com.

Loose parts could include:

- Tree cookies (1/2" to 1" slices of various sized branches)

- Old discarded CDs/DVDs
- 1-2 inch diameter tree branch sections, preferably cut so they will stand up
- Glass "blobs" (a dollar store purchase)
- Flowers (real or "silk")
- Fabric of various sizes
- Popsicle sticks or tongue depressors
- Rocks
- Strips of bark and interesting branch pieces
- Shells
- Scraps of wood from a building site (be careful that the pieces are smooth enough and not treated with chemicals)
- Unspun wool in various colors such as Momoda Felting Materials can be found on Amazon.com.
- Found materials
- Packing forms (like what furniture comes packaged in)
- Anything that comes into the house that might be conducive to building, including:
  - plastic bottle tops
  - small plastic jars
  - shells
  - popsicle sticks
  - empty thread spools
  - tubes that come inside doggie poop bags
  - small bits of netting
  - anything small and reflective (little mirror squares, aluminum foil)
  - heavy cardboard tubes of various lengths

Use what you have and your imagination!

Window Wonders

- Fasmov transparent colored plastic can be found on Amazon.com.

Creating a qr code for your child's portfolio

Steps for putting a video in your child's portfolio

- Upload your video to youtube or vimeo
- Copy the url for your video
- Open a qr code generator such as: https://www.the-qrcode-generator. com/
- Paste the url into the generator
- Right click on and copy the qr code that is generated
- Paste into Word, Pages, or other app that allows you to print a document
- Print the qr code for your child's portfolio

Mommy, they're taking away my imagination!

Acknowledgments

I humbly thank all the children I taught over 37 years and their parents for going on this journey of learning with me. They were and will always be my teachers.

I am so grateful to Dory Doyle and Dorothy Suskind for supporting me through the process of writing and editing! Their kind reading has made this a much better book.

Thank you to my young friends Audrey and David. Their imagination is immense and inspiring.

I will always be grateful to the educators of Reggio Emilia for giving me an image of what early childhood education should be.

Thanks to my husband, Larry, for his patience when I got in the flow of writing and ignored him, and for trying to keep the dogs quiet while I wrote.

And most of all, thank you to my mother, Mary Lou, who was instrumental in helping Tristan keep his imagination safe.

References

Carson, Rachel. *The Sense of Wonder.* New York: Harper and Row, 1965. p 20.

Dewey, John. "Self-Realization as the Moral Ideal" *Philosophical Review* 2 (6):652-664 (1893)

Loris Malaguzzi. History, ideas and basic philosophy: An interview with Lella Gandini in Edwards, C., L. and Forman, G. (Eds.) *The hundred languages of children: The Reggio Emilia Experience in Transformation.* Santa Barbara, CA: Praeger. 2012. p 57 and p 44.

Loris Malaguzzi. *The Catalog of the 100 Languages of Children Exhibit.* Reggio Children. 1996.

Oken-Wright, Pam. "Embracing Snow." In Hendrick, J. *Next Steps Toward Teaching The Reggio Way.* Upper Saddle River, NJ: Merrill Prentice Hall. pp 175-194.

Rinaldi, Carla. www.facebook.com/REA.Interest.Group

Rosin, Hanna. "The Overprotected Kid" *The Atlantic.* April 2014.

"Socrates on Education" StudyMode.com. 05 2011. 2011. 05 2011 <https://www.studymode.com/essays/Socrates-On-Education-704821.html>

For Further Reading

Christakis, Erika. *The Importance of Being Little: What Preschoolers Really Need from Grownups.* New York: Viking, 2016.

Compton, Michelle and Thompson, Robin. *Story Making: The Maker Movement Approach to Literacy for Early Learners.* Redleaf Press. 2018.

Edwards, Carolyn, Gandini, Lella, and Forman, George, eds. *The Hundred Languages of Children: The Reggio Emilia Experience in Transformation.* 3rd edition. Santa Barbara, CA: Praeger, 2012.

Gopnik, Alison, Meltzoff, Andrew, and Kuhl, Patricia. *The Scientist in the Crib: Minds, Brains, and How Children Learn.* New York: William Morrow and Co, 1999.

Kolbe, Ursula. *Children's Imagination: Creativity Under Our Noses.* Peppinot Press. 2014.

Oken-Wright, Pam. http://pokenwright.com/the-voices-of-children-blog/

Topal, Cathy, *Beautiful Stuff! Learning with Found Materials.* Worcester, Mass: Davis Publications,1999.

CPSIA information can be obtained
at www.ICGtesting.com
Printed in the USA
BVHW022104100820
586076BV00014B/379